CIRCLE
OF
HOPE

DANIELLA SEYMOUR

Ordering Information:

Prime Seven Media
518 Landmann St.
Tomah City, WI 54660

Printed in the United States of America

TABLE OF CONTENTS

CHAPTER 1

My earliest memory is when my mum was at the pub and me and my twin sister Stef and my older sister Tracy were standing at the garden gate. We were worried and crying at the gate. My Mum, due to the stresses of life and upset in her life, was an alcoholic. We loved our mum very much. She was one of the seven children. I always remember my mum as being very beautiful, but full of hurt. I was three years old that night.

At this point, my mum was on her own looking after three young children. My parents had split up, but my mum did not want to accept this – she was still in love with my father. My parents met when my Father was in the army and my Mum wrote letters to him. A lot of young women did this at the time. My Father was from Bassett in Southampton. My grandparents from my Dad's side were from Ireland.

My Father was a good looking man –women would always try to get with my Father. This made my Mum jealous, as it would do anyone.

Both my parent drank, which made matters worse. They were lovely people before a drink, but turned into nasty people once had a few. People drink when they are upset or just to have fun with friends.

But too much drink can cause a lot of upset to yourself and people around you. No one is the same person when drinking alcohol. It doesn't matter how much you think you are, you are NOT in control, believe me, you are not.

I have good memories also, of cooking toast on our fire and having a bath in the sink (th sink used to be a lot bigger back then). This was before I was five years old. So we were not that big anyway. Also, I remember my mum would sing and rub our heads at night until we fell asleep. ('We' being myself and my two sisters.)

When I was five years old my mum married my stepfather George. He was previously married with three children. His ex-wife died a number of years before he met my Mother. But before then, myself, Stef and Tracy had to go into care.

I can remember one day the social worker, a nice lady, she took us away from our Mother. I can remember sitting in the back of the car screaming and crying for my mother, harder and harder out of the back of the window as she become smaller and smaller, then gone. It still can upset me to this day, but yet I was three years old and I can still remember the pain caused when I was taken away from my Mother.

I don't know where we were in care, but I do remember an old house. It was a lovely house with big glass doors. I also remember sitting in front of this large old fireplace, I think it might have been Christmas, as I can remember something around the fire place but can't remember what.

But my sisters and I were with an old lady who had white hair in a bun at the back of her head. We were all drinking hot milk. To this day I don't know who that was or where it was.

But I can also remember sitting in a big room where my mum and father used to come and see me and my sisters, but then we would be crying for them not to go. But they had to. I did not understand at this time – it was before I was 5 years old.

When my mother met George my stepfather, it was in the butcher's shop across the road from where we lived. My mother went across a lot, either to have a chat or do her hair. But yes this is where they first met.

When my mum married George, he helped her get us out of care. Myself and my twin sister stayed with our mother, and Tracy went to live with my father in Southampton.

I can still remember the day my mum and my stepdad got married. Myself and my sister were dressed in cream dresses with pretty brown flowers on, and the frills were very pretty. We were dressed and we were waiting an hour before it was time to go. We were so excited. That hour went so slow, one of the longest hours in my life. My stepfather loved my mum so much – if she wanted something, she got it, she always did, even when my mum was screaming at him to get more sherry, he would do what my mother asked for. Or he would just say no, enough is enough and just sit down, he never raised his voice once. Even though she could be nasty when drunk, he still loved every hair on her body.

We travelled each year to visit our dad. He always came to pick us up at stoke station and also brought us back. The joy every time we saw him was great – our dad! Myself and my sister would run to him. We would try to watch for his train to get in, but when it was busy you could not always see who got off the train on the other side of the station, before they would walk down the stairs to the exit. So me and Stef would always look at the faces in the crowd to see our Dad. We would run to him and he always put one of us on his shoulders. My God it was scary for me, because my Dad was very tall. I would be scared but then get used to it because I was safe with my Dad, he would make sure we did not get hurt.

But between these visits my Mum would drink, all my life I have known my Mum to drink constantly, every day for weeks at a time. But there's drinking and drinking. Only my Mum used to drink QC sherry, non-stop so she could not walk or talk just drink go to sleep, drink and go to sleep.

I can remember when George came to pick us up from primary school, and I said to him: "Where's my Mum, is she drunk again? Because she's an alcoholic" I don't think he could believe his ears. We stopped walking and he said: "Please don't say that about your Mother, she is just unwell."

I never did say it again, but I did think it.

At the age of nine years old. I remember being in the kitchen talking to my Mum when there was a knock on the door. It was a policeman. He asked to speak to my parents first and then he went. Me and Stef wondered what was going on. Why did the policeman come?

My Stepdad explained to us that our real Dad, Desmond Beach, had died of a stabbing in the leg on his main vein and he bled to death. It was at his birthday party and a neighbor complained about the noise and we got told there was an argument. The people at the party did not realize my Dad had gone but when they did, it was too late. He bled out a lot and was hardly alive. He died in the ambulance on the way to the hospital.

I can remember it like it was yesterday. I just sat there. I did not cry even though Stef did straight away. I just sat there and stared at Stef while she was crying. When our Dad died our school life changed, from being in the top classes to being in the lowest. This affected our school lives so much.

From the age of five we used to help our Stepdad with my Mum when she was drunk. I can remember like it was yesterday. My Mum fell off the settee asleep and she bit the inside of her mouth. There was a lot of blood and I was scared. I got lots of tissues for my Mum and water to rinse it off. I could not stop crying. I thought my Mum was going to die. When you see a lot of blood, it can scare anybody.

When I was cleaning up the blood my Mum would just look at me, and I would try to help the best way I could, but the stare my Mum would give was a woman in pain. But then she could change in seconds and start shouting at my Stepdad to get more QC sherry. If my Stepdad said no, God it was world war three. It was not nice to see.

I considered it normal when my Mum drank, due to the fact that was all I had seen, all my life. When my Mum would drink she would cry, and say her sisters won't talk to her and she misses her Dad and she loved my real Dad still and it hurts that he did not feel the same way. She would continue with this On and off, it made me upset seeing my Mum cry like this.

Sometimes I would try to cheer my Mum up. If I knew I could. My Mum would calm down, have another drink and go back to sleep. Everybody took my Mum to the toilet, some people more than others.

Stef was a selfish sister, yes she helped, but only when it suited her. I can remember not going to school because I was helping my Stepdad. I would lose friends because I could not go out and leave my Stepdad to everything on his own. It was really upsetting. All my life it was always upsetting. My Stepdad loved my Mum very much, he knew she was hurting, even when she shouted at him saying she did not love him and she hated him and she loves Desmond Beach and always will.

I felt for my Stepdad when she said it, she would shout it at the top of her voice too. It was quite scary at times. Sometimes my Mum would start drinking because her sisters would park outside of the house to go the shops opposite where we lived. Sometimes we wished — and I think my Mum would too — that we would hear a knock on the door. But no, it was not to be, no more than five times can I remember seeing the family when we were little. It was not fair. We could not visit our family like other families do. My Mum missed her sisters so much. My Mum would get upset also saying: "Our Nan, she would buy gifts and give cards to other grandkids but she did not with us." Me and my sisters was used to this.

I can't remember anything I ever had from my Nan Leigh for any birthday or at Christmas. Me and my sisters would get upset because we thought our family did not care or like us. Which started my Mum drinking, sometimes, because my Mum would be staring out of the window just hoping they might come in after going to the shop. One out of thirty times they did. I missed my family so much and think it would have been lovely to have a family. It would have given us a bit more confidence. Still to this day I'm a stranger to my cousins.

Hardly know any of them, this I feel is unfair, we did not do anything wrong. Me and my sister that is.

We got told when were younger that there was an argument between the family and my Mum and something to do with my Stepfather. But he worshiped the ground my Mum walked on, always did. Always! When we would go shopping, God if my Mum wanted something, he would buy it for her straight away, or sometimes which was really nice. He would wait for their first cup of tea. From when we got back in the house and my Stepdad would say, "Oh by the way" to my Mum, and pass her the gift.

I used to think it was sweet of him. He always did the cooking; I can only remember my Mum cooking two or three times in my life. My Mum would mop everywhere every day. My Mum was a very clean person as was my Stepdad.

My Mum could be very spiteful person, because she was unhappy. She said if she was unhappy, everyone was. I can't remember having a good relationship with my Mum ever until I moved out. I felt like my Mum all my life loved Stef a lot more than me. Stef was her favorite. It was not until her last Christmas she was alive when she said sorry for this.

She said it was because I was a lot stronger than Stef. I hugged my Mum and wanted to cry when she said it, I said it was OK. It was lovely when she said it and I felt closer to my Mum than ever before in my life.

But looking after my Mum when she was drinking all my life I think it was unfair. I would look after her and not even get any thanks, because she just turned back to being spiteful again. I can remember once I told my Mum a bit about myself, and that day 1 treasured because it was nice to get on with my Mum. But then a week after she called me a slag because of what I told her. It was about my first boyfriend. 1 treasured that day after talking to my Mum. But it only lasted a week. I would always try to build up a relationship with my Mum but it would be so hard most of the time.

One Christmas Eve I had no money to get my Mum a present, so I did a babysitting job and I hated these people. But I did it so I could give my Slum something. I thought it was better than nothing. I felt so proud of myself. I was happy at the end of the night because I could actually give my Mum something. I had nothing but did something about it. For my Mum. But she was pissed off with me on Christmas morning and got angry at me. She said: "How dare you insult me like this."

I could not believe my ears. She said because of the way I treated her, I only got half of the Christmas money that she was going to give me and my twin sister for Christmas. I was so upset.

I did not realize how nasty she could be. Even without a drink. There was no way I could have gone to a shop, because it was Christmas Eve. It was lam when I got back in. I begged to her saying I was not being funny, but there were no shops open. She said "Tough". She did not care.

She had to be number one top dog in the house and she liked if you groveled to her, in other words, "lick my feet and then I shall decide to forgive you or not". But why? I did not think that way. I just wanted to give my Slum something nice. I did not want to hurt my

Mum, far from it, I hated my Mum for this, I just wanted a Mum to get on with.

Once there was a competition I wanted to enter, but I needed Sellotape for the envelope. All my Mum had to do, when I asked for it, saying please and everything, was unlock the cupboard and get it. She knew what she was doing, she pretended that she could not find the keys so that she could not find the Sellotape.

She knew that this meant a lot to me, but she did not care. She would smile like a wicked witch. Well, if she did not act like a wicked witch all my life I would not call her one. If my Mum was unhappy, she would take it out on you. All my life she was like this. WHY WHY WHY? It's unfair.

This is only a tiny bit of what my Mum was like, she always had to get her own way. Sad or what? My Mum would let my sister go on day trips with her friends and even go on holiday. But only one out of ten times I asked was it a yes for me. I felt left out all my life, I never felt loved.

With my Mum being the way she was, I never felt good enough to be loved. My Mum has affected me all my life. If she had more love to show me and hadn't told me "you are worthless or stupid and thick" I would have felt happy and secure in life. Not like I'm not good enough for anything or anyone. I can remember crying, crying a lot, as a child.

Me and my sister did not have brand names but clothes just good enough, my Stepdad was very old fashioned. They did their best. We looked like boys when we were younger, with a basin haircut. When everyone had a BMX we had a scooter, which you had to push along with your foot. I did love to go up and down the garden though. We were grateful whatever we had. But I feel any child wants more than what they got, so I feel unfair to my Mum and Stepdad.

When you get older, as a teenager, you need have nice stuff or you get bullied, by the time you get to high school (which I never went to the last two years, because we felt like tramps). I used to love dancing. My PE teacher ran a dance team and asked if I wanted to join. I was so happy, but not for long. I realized that my parents did not have money to buy things. So I never asked them. So that went out of the window. I was so happy, yet again, but not for long. Dancing was my dream, yeah right, splat bang, my dreams stamped on as usual.

CHAPTER 2

Being a teenager

By the time I was 13 years old, I got myself a paper round and babysitting job. I learnt in life that nothing comes free and you had to work for it. My twin sister Stef used to nick some of my money from my coat pocket. I would tell my Mum and she said it was my own fault that I left it in there. She got away with something else again! She is heartless and always has been. My twin sister is still a selfish person, she always was and always will be. So I decided to do the same to her, just to see what happens, but I decided to put the money in the bathroom window.

So I waited until Stef had money. When she did I went in to her pocket and took it, not all of it. I just wanted to prove a point, to my Mum and myself. So I pretended to nick it, and put it in the bathroom window. My Mum really told me off because I went in her pocket, So I said to her: "You see, when I leave money in my pocket it's alright if she nicks it, but when I do it, it's a different matter!" I said I did not nick it. It's in the bathroom window. My point was proven! I can't even remember what my Mum said. Tell you the truth,

I did not really care. Stef was a mummy's girl, got her own way too much.

The hardest thing in life, is to live it. It does not matter what happened to you in life. You are always in control of the person you become, there is no excuse for causing another person pain or suffering, so life was still looking after my Mum when drunk and being upset because why can't life be different? Why could I not have a Mum who would not act selfishly and a sister who was not selfish. It Would have been nice to have a family and to get on.

At 14-and-a-half years I met my first boyfriend who I had sexual contact with. We got on great. He was about two years older than me. He had two brothers and a sister. I got on with his mum too. It was a nice family, they made me feel welcome. I was with him nearly a year. When three days before my 15th birthday, I complained to my Mum that I had a really bad stomach. She told me to just go to bed.

"Thanks

Mum!" I thought.

Anyway, I did what I was told and went to bed. I was then woken up by my Stepdad asking me if I was alright. I was covered in blood. If it was not for my Stepdad checking on me, I would have bled to death.

I slept on a double bed with two mattresses on, and my blood went through both of them. It was a very scary time for me. I was rushed to hospital. By the time I got to hospital, I don't remember a thing. I woke up the next day in a hospital bed. I had a miscarriage. I tried to go to the toilet but could not stand, because it made me dizzy. I lost a lot of blood. My Mum and Stepdad were very kind, and looked happy when I woke up. I can remember my Mum saying: "You nearly made me another grandparent!"

A week after I came out of hospital I had an argument and my Mum called me a slag. I could not believe it, she hurt me so much already in life, and she did it more and more, until I left home at 16 years.

At 16 years old I did not know what to do, I didn't any qualifications because I hadn't been to school for the last two years. I got bullied twice that was it. I could not go back to school at that point of my life I had enough of feeling like a tramp. Me and my sister did not have any trainers and had to borrow plimsoles, very embarrassing, so I could not cope with it. My mum, being drunk half the time, then when she did not drink, she was being spiteful, I could not win. So I did not go to school for the last two years.

At 16 years I was not sure what to do with my life, I went to the job Centre and started a YTS course (Youth Training Scheme). Stef started as well. I started to do pottery, but did not like it that much. So I started the Business Administration course.

The training scheme lasted for two years only, and by the time I finished I had done level 1 and 2 and three-quarters of level 3. I enjoyed Business Administration, but it was hard at first. But when you are doing something that you enjoy, you do it better and learn quicker.

Meanwhile in the two years I did the training I had two boyfriends, and had fun. But these two years of my life (ages 16—18) would be the only two years in my life I actually enjoyed. The only two years in my life to have fun and be free to do what I wanted.

I already decided to try to do what I could in my life. I did not smoke or drink or take drugs. My sister Stef smoked from the age of 12 or 13 years old. I was the quiet twin in a way. With twins there is a good one (which is me) and then a bad one which was Stef. I've come to realize, that with a lot of twins, the first one born is the good one and the second born is the naughty one.

We started the YTS course. It was the first week and the salary was 05, and I always dreamed of getting my hair permed. I had seen girls at school and they would look very pretty with their curly hair. So I remember going to the hairdressers in town and asking how much it was. It was 05. I thought, what was I going to say to my Mum, what I did with the first week's rent money! Ah!

I went to have my hair permed. God, I thought it was great. My Mum did not when she was holding out her hand while I just pointed to my hair. I think I laughed only a little. My Mum, therefore, was not a happy lady! Never mind I thought. . . ah!

I met with an old friend whose name was Kerry. We started going to a night club in town. We would go every Tuesday night. It was great! The first time we went I went in a top with shoulder pads in. We so looked like first timers! It was funny. I hung that top up, and I don't think I wore it again.

Me and Kerry started gaining in confidence, and we would dance a lot. Mainly all night. I loved dancing. We also built our confidence with the men. We would go with enough money to get in, that was all. The night club had three rooms, with different music in each room. We would chat to a man to get us a drink, drink it and then walk off into another room. We did this for a few months. Then we both started to see these two friends, who both lived a bit out of town. I went to see Troy every weekend his family made me feel welcome. He lived with his older sister and a younger sister who was 15 years old. had a good relationship at first, but he started to try to tell me what to do, so started to see this other guy who D]. it was cool going places, he would and I Ad dance and dance and dance away till the end he night.

I did not realize that they would be the last two years I ever enjoyed.

CHAPTER 3

I moved back into my Slum's after a year, just for a 1little while
at 18 years old. I didn't know what to do with my life, I was
just sitting in my bedroom a lot. My Mum would be spiteful
as ever. She made me feel like I was nothing, I'm not good enough,
I'm not even a person. Why did she have to act this way?

I was one person in the house and another outside the gates. My
Mum used to make me feel low, so with my friends I would always try
to act cheerful when really inside I was crying for help. I felt I always
had to feel like I had to try and act like I was happy because you don't
want a friend who's always depressed. In the house, I was quiet and
felt sad, a little bit of love would have been nice.

If you were unhappy my Mum seemed to be happy. She was
strange like that, you want the best for your kids, but not my Mum.
I was not working at the time, when I moved back in with my Mum.
There was a problem with my money and I did not get paid at all,
but I gave my belongings to my Mum to cover the rent. My Mum was
fine with this. But when my back pay came through from the Social,
I had to give my Mum three-quarters of the money. Otherwise I
would be kicked out, and she wanted to go on holiday. I had already

paid her, but she said I had not and started to cry to get her own way. I will never forget that, and never will, she was always cruel, which she liked to do, to make herself feel better and to feel good about herself.

I could go on and on but what is the point, it won't make the problem go away. I don't want to mislead anyone to thinking I did not love my Mum - I did, I always will but it was not until I got older that I would understand more about my Slum and the upset and pain she was in. She always wanted to die, to be with my Dad. She would say this in front of my Stepdad too, and if she was drinking she would say it again to make sure he heard it properly. My mum always could be nasty when she had a drink. It was good when she went to sleep.

One day when I was nearly 18 years old, I realized I had to get up and try to do something with my life. I had to. I had to try. So I tried to do something about it. I went to my old friend, Kerry, and asked if she would like to go out on the Tuesday I got paid, she said yes. I thought great! I was proud I did something instead of sitting there bored. I also signed up to go in the NAAFI.

I had things to look forward to. Stef had a boyfriend called Lee. One night she came back to me and said he had a friend who would like to meet me. Lee had told his friend Peter) that Stef had a twin sister. So I went with Stef one night, around to her boyfriend's flat, it was at the bottom of the estate, half-an-hour walk. But the night I went he did not turn up. I did not realize at the time he was seeing someone else, and the night he was supposed to meet me she turned up at his house to surprise him. So he could not come to meet me!

The next day I was going to sign on to get my money, and Stef said come with her to Lee's flat and we can sign on after. SVC had enough time she said and his friend Peter might be there too.

So I went with Stef and this Peter guy was there. got on great. He wasn't long out of jail— two weeks before. He was a burglar, but stole from the rich not the poor. A burglar with morals! I thought he was a nice guy to talk to, he had brown eyes. I liked brown, yes. Mmm, I thought and wondered. He also had love bites and I still had not realized this about him. Love is blind! (That's my excuse and I'm keeping to it!)

A week after starting a relationship with Peter, I had to go to Manchester to take an exam to get in to the NAAFI. But my Mum would not help me with the cost of getting there and if I spent what I had I would have nothing still for another week and a half. So I never went to take the exam. I NEVER had support from my Mum and Stepdad. It always had to be the hard way or no way.

If my parents had helped when I needed it, it would have taken me down another road of life, a much better one. As for the one I went down, you never know, is it destiny what you've got though? Is everything for a reason? Is your life already set for you? Why could I not have a family? A husband? A life?

I try to think life is only what you make it. But some things that happen you can't control. You try to think, or even pretend you are in control, but the truth is far from than that. You are looking for love, but there isn't any love to find. There is only the circle of hope.

Two weeks into the relationship, it was Peter's birthday. I did not give him anything except a card, but within these two weeks we already had our first argument, because of a remark somebody made about me because they thought I was pretty. This made Peter jealous but he treated it as if it was my fault. I should have known it was bad to have an argument within two weeks. But no, I loved him already, only if I thought then how he acted within the first two weeks I should have really stopped the relationship there, but no, I had to learn the hard way. Sometimes your heart tells you one thing but your head tells you another, which one you go down, can be a very hard decision. But it was not hard for me, I chose the wrong road. If only I had a bit more support in my life from my parents, well who knows! It was not my parents' fault even though I made it sound that way, it was my own.

Well I got my flat and Peter was happy, because we had a flat and not just his bedroom. but from the beginning Peter was in control of everything, I did not know anything about having my own home. But Peter already had a house with an ex of his. He made me feel so stupid because I did not know simple things about my own home. But I loved him so at this point.

God I thought he was really clever and sexy too!

We lived two separate lives, it felt like. Love I thought is where you care for someone, make sure they are alright and happy enough. No, not for me. Love was used as a weapon — if you love me, do what you are told and keep me happy or else! That is what love was like for me. I dreamt to be happy. I love him till the end of time. Why this? He could not see the tears and my heartache. But he could see the bruises he gave me, and all he would say is "sorry, I did not mean to hit you. I promise it won't happen again," and then he would hold me in his arms. I would think it's you, it's always you, everything I do is for you. But never had the courage to.

It did not matter how much he hurt me physically, I always forgave him, because I loved him and hoped that one day he would change if I carried on doing what I'm told. It will make him happy and hopefully he might stop hurting me.

Peter told me he did not have a good childhood, and that is why he was like he was, because he didn't want to get hurt in life because he had been hurt enough. Even though it was not my fault, I always tried to make up for his childhood. To make up for his bad times in life.

I was so in love with him. I thought he was so beautiful and good hearted, even though he hurt me. That didn't matter, when we first met, we got on so much, I thought it was magical, to me anyway. But the more money he had, he changed, He was far from the person I met where did my Peter go?

Peter was going out every night and drinking every night. I would stand and iron his clothes for him every night. Peter was getting more and more distant from me. I started to think he was going with some other woman. Our personal life was few and far between. peter would tell me I'm not good enough for him and I don't look after myself. So if he went out and two timed me, it was all my fault. This was heart breaking to hear.

When Peter came back at night or in the early hours, he would start on me for being ugly. How on earth he started a relationship with me he would never know. Then he would get angrier, and then he would hit me and kick me. He would get harder. I would beg him and say I would start to look after myself properly and please forgive me.

I would be standing there with a black eye; my body would be hurting so much. He would hit me on my head as well. Everywhere on my body because not one part of my body was good enough for him and I deserved him hitting me. It was all my own fault.

I started to look after myself because I was dirty and disgusting. I didn't deserve to be loved. I would cry so much, I never told anyone what he was doing, because I was embarrassed. I believed I deserved to be hit, and I would hide the fact. If we had any visitors he would act so nice, as if life is full of roses. As time went by I got more low. I had no confidence. What was that? As soon as the visitors left, Peter would go back to his usual self. I would beg for him to talk to me. But no, I was not good enough. Nothing I did was ever good enough. Then the time of day would come where I would be standing there again ironing his clothes to go out in. When ironing his clothes if only one bit was not ironed properly he would make me iron it all again and hit me for being so thick. I can't even iron a shirt or jeans or anything in fact, he would shout. Then he would go out and I would be left in all night on my own, then he would come back drunk and hit me again and then the next morning he would say sorry and I would forgive him again. The circle of hope I called it, over and over again, this would happen. Around and around we would go.

I thought when you love someone it means you care for them and you will be happy. Why does love have to hurt so much? Why can't you love someone and they love you back? Why has it got to be full of pain instead? More pain and more pain! On and on and on! If love hurts this much, then is it love? Or obsession or pretence?

Then if this is love then why do I feel so empty? So lost? So scared? So lonely? So stupid?

But when I told the council I was expecting a baby to get the flat, I did not realize I really was pregnant. As a few months went by, I knew I could not tell Peter. I was too scared to.

Weeks went past, and I thought if I did not talk about the problem. it may go away. But it did not. Every night in the bath I would talk to my stomach and rub my stomach. I would talk to my stomach like it was going to talk back to me, I did not know what to do. J cried and cried and cried.

Peter already told me I was not good enough to be with him and he would never allow me to have a baby. I did not know what to do, I thought of leaving him. I decided to tell Peter. He looked at me, really angry, and said: "GET RID OF IT OR GO."

He said it like I was a tramp and he was a prince. J never forgot the hurt when he said those words. I just went to my bedroom and cried enough to make an ocean.

I made an appointment with my doctor to discuss the matter. I had to have a scan because the doctor said it is not a normal abortion because I was nearly five months, he/she was a whole baby and I had to get rid of it like it was nothing. A life is not nothing, especially when it's inside of you. I just agreed everything with the doctor. I don't even think I heard what he said. I just knew I was doing what I was told. I went home and tried not to think about it.

But every night in the bath, before I was due to go to the hospital, I just cried and cried. I kept telling my baby, "Sorry, I'm so sorry and I will miss you and I love you". I asked my baby to forgive me, and that it was not my fault this was happening, and that I had no choice. Sitting in the bath holding my stomach, holding my baby, begging with him/her to forgive me please, please!

I had to say goodbye to my unborn baby because Peter would not let me keep him/her. I was not allowed to keep my baby. I was not good enough to be a mother. As well, in my eyes because that is what Peter said, "I'm useless, I'm stupid, I can't look after myself never mind a baby. You thick cow. A baby, you? You are just a dumbo." He told me people made fun of me also, because "You can't even talk properly, you can't walk properly either, you don't do anything properly. I would feel embarrassed if you were a mother to a kid of mine."

I had every day and got beaten up every night. When he came back in drunk, he told me I'm not good enough for anything, everything and nothing. used to watch his face when I was standing there scared stiff. He used to hit me like he hated me, like I had done something wrong, I had to beg for mercy till he stopped hitting me, and talk to him, tell him I agreed with what he said and tried to cheer the mood up, so he stopped getting angry and hitting me again. Every day, every night it went on till I went to the hospital, to get rid of it. He was so happy when I told him about going to the hospital, I could not believe it, I made him happy but what I had to do to make him happy with mc was destroying me. It was me who had to go through with it.

After I told Peter about the hospital, he told me I had to tell our parents. I had to tell both parents what was happening the day before I had to go in, I went to my parents first and went to his Dad and his Stepmom after. But on my own. He made me tell them on my own.

After telling my Mum and Stepdad I walked out of the door, out the gate and marched to his parents, talking to my baby all the way and holding my stomach. I just knew I was doing what I was told by Peter. I had to keep Peter happy, I thought.

Well the morning arrived, I had to go to hospital to get rid of my baby. I felt empty. Why could I not keep my baby? Peter took me to the hospital, and dropped me off. I went in alone. I had to go on a ward, where I had my own room. I thought that was cool. But it's because of what you go through — you have to give birth to a dead baby, which I help to get rid of. It was not my choice; I was just doing what I was told. Hal an hour after being there Peter came back with some flowers (that's very kind, I thought). I showed him the papers about what I had to go through. To make a Jong story short, I had to take three tablets. I can still remember taking them. I felt like a murderer, After Peter left I just sat on the bed in my room. I felt like I was doing this for Peter. I did not realize what I was about to go through. Did not realize I had to give birth to the baby I helped to kill. My heart was going 100mph, I needed a fag. I was just about to go for a fag when my Mum walked through the door wow, thank you Mum!

I feel so alone and when my Mum came in, I felt like my Mum knew I did not really want to go through with it. My Mum knew Peter was hitting me. I really thought I was doing the best thing, and because Peter told mc to, I thought it would not be fair to bring a baby into the world, especially because Peter kept hitting me. Well me and my Mum went down to the smoking room, but first of all I had to take the first tablet. They were quite big, I swallowed the tablet like I was taking a headache tablet. We got to the smoking room with our cup of tea each. I must have smoked a hundred fags. I was very quiet, hardly speaking to my Mum, except to say, "Thank you for supporting me, for coming."

A few hours went by and I was on the third tablet. Visiting hours were up soon. So we went into the smoking room, and I just sat there crying. I did NOT want to kill my baby. I was so upset. My Mum knew why I was there in this situation, because of Peter. My Mum kept telling me the reasons why I was doing this, she repeated the reasons I told her the day before. But J did not mean them. I was just doing what I was told by Peter. So I just took the tablet and cried really hard. This is not fair. I remember thinking this will make Peter happy. I don't think I realized what I did till after, I felt like I could not even talk. The nurse told me it will be a few hours later when the baby will come out, I still did not realize. I felt like something was wrong so I rang the bell, It felt like blood a water came flooding out of me. I had to push a few times to help the baby come out.

I said I did not want to know the sex, everything was too much for me. My baby was gone, taken from me and he/she had to be buried. I gave a name to both sexes. I hurt so much. Please God forgive me, I did not want to do this. I was made to. But I did have a choice, which I did not realize at the time. It was the next morning. Peter was coming to pick me up from the hospital. He came and he looked so happy, it was like a big weight off his shoulders. I could not believe it. But I could not say my point of few, I was too scared to.

That night I went for a bath, when Peter went out as usual, I must have been in the bath for a few hours. I could not stop crying in the bath, holding my stomach wanting my baby back, begging please

God! All I ever knew in life was heartache, time and time and time again. Please God, no more.

Me and Peter never really spoke about it again. All I had was a scan. The nurses wondered why I wanted a scan if I was getting rid of it? I think they came to realize that it was because I did NOT want to get rid of it. All I had of my baby was a scan. It was not fair.

I woke up the next morning and just carried on, tried to push my baby to the back of my mind. I came to think if I don't think about it or talk about it, it did not happen. I tried to pretend to myself it was just a dream; it did not really happen. Peter had three other kids, Lewis was his youngest, he was only three. Peter had him one day a week.

The next morning his son was due to come and it was Mother's Day. Peter told me I had go the shop and get a Mother's Day card for Lewis, to give to his Mum. My heart stopped beating, Did I really hear those words come from his mouth?

I had no choice and I had to get one, I walked down to the shop, I cried all the way third and back.

I picked a lovely card, a card I would have liked to have had if I was a mother.

I did not say anything when I came back from the shop, I just carried on and on, I was not allowed to have an opinion, I could not talk about it at all. I could not make decisions around the home, Peter controlled everything.

His brother would come to pick him up and there were three people in the car. His brother would drive, and his girlfriend would sit in the front seat and there another girl at the back. Who was that,

I thought? I knew, but never admitted it to myself. How dare Peter bring his girlfriend to our home and do that in front of my face. He did not care. I was nothing to him. That would happen a lot.

Day in day out I kept myself busy and stopped eating properly. I did not want to eat. I was punishing myself and also I stopped going out. I just stayed in. I looked at myself and thought that I was ugly, dirty and nasty. I was getting sick of it.

One morning when Peter hit me, I hit him back on his face, He was gobsmacked. I think I was too. I just stood there and covered my mouth and said, "Oh no!" Peter got me back and hit me harder for slapping him and so J would not do it again. He tried to teach me a lesson. But I was used to getting hurt, feeling pain all the time was normal to me. Having bruises or my head hurting because Peter kicked me on my head, well in fact he used to hit and kick me anywhere on my body, it did not matter to him.

The hardest thing in life is to live it. Many people have gone through hurt and pain and because of it have suffered, or are still suffering, with depression It does NOT matter what has happened in your life You are in control of the person you become.

I always made excuses for Peter, and believed in my head that he would change one day. If I just stayed around and did what he said, he would come to realize that I do really love him. I will prove it to him. The circle of hope, what a circle it is. You don't realize it's YOU who is in control of that circle, NO one else. But realizing it is NOT a simple matter.

When the man you love so much is hitting you kicking you, all you think is when will he stop. The pain of each hit you don't really feel till he has stopped. You sit and cry, why me, I do really love him, God I do, you mentally think he must be right, because why else would he hit me? You beg and plead and do anything you can to calm him down. But if he was drunk and fell asleep, I used to think "Hooray, he sleeping". I would stare at him while he was asleep He was very beautiful to me. He looked such a nice person when he was asleep. What a shame he wakes up and the day starts off again, repeatedly, time aft time and time again.

I would iron his clothes every night making sur I had ironed carefully and properly. Otherwise would shout. But while I was ironing, I would stand and think and wonder what the girl looks like when he goes out in these clothes? When Peter got out the bath he would put the clothes on I just ironed. Wishing and thinking that he looked so nice and smelled so nice, why couldn't he do this for me?

Peter knew and I knew he was going with other women. We would not talk about it, only when he came back pissed. Depending upon how drunk he was, he would shout and say, "Why couldn't you look after yourself, you always look like a tramp?" And he would hit me blah blah and more blah!

Once he came back drunk and went for a wee in the corner of the room, it was so funny. If it was somebody else, he would have gone mad. But I had great pleasure telling him in the morning when he woke up. He would wake up when he pleased.

He used to wake up and say, "Who hit you?"

I would say, "You."

He would say, "Sorry, I was drunk, I won't do it again. You do know I love you, right?"

I would say, "Of course you do."

Yeah right, in my head I would be calling him every name I could.

Sometimes at night I would cry myself to sleep, and then be woken up when he come back in, I was so lonely, I would sit with my dog and I would cover him up, I even would give him a pillow. I would sit there in the out place with my dog, and cry and talk and cry and talk. My dog would just look at me. He seemed to understand what I was saying, but couldn't talk back. He would just look at me, he was gorgeous and my best friend. I loved him so much. Once he was in the living room with us and Peter hit me. The dog jumped up and went to bite him. Peter kicked him a couple of times, he yelped and it really made me upset, He was only trying to protect me and he got kicked because of it. I couldn't stop crying. I thought, "Thank you mate!" But I did not want him to get-hurt because of me.

When I was sitting on my own at night, I would think, what do I have to do to prove to him I love him? When I proved it to him he will stop me then. So every day I lived for him, to make him happy. If he said jump I said, "how high?" If I made him happy, he will stop hurting me. He will! I know he will.

People can bring on misery in their lives, but you need to fight it, not let it win. Life, the hardest thing is to live it. Why keep bringing misery on? Push it away, don't give it a helping hand. Live life, be happy and be free of domestic violence or any kind of abuse. You can do it. You think you can't but you can. DO IT, BE STRONG, BE FREE. PLEASE DO IT FOR YOURSELF.

It was nearly Christmas 1994. I knew I would not be celebrating. I could not do anything, like Peter would. But I had a friend around the corner. On Christmas Eve I went to her house. Not for too long, but we had three or four shots of whisky and we were singing in the street after, while walking back to my flat. I wore a really nice dress, it was beautiful. But when we both got around to my flat Peter was not very happy with me. I thought, God I could not remember the last time I laughed. It was great. But no Peter always spoiled everything for me. He destroyed everything that made me happy. He did not like me being happy, no that was against the law in his book.

My friend went because of Peter and he started to shout at me, He said, "What do you think you are doing? You look like a tart!"

The dress was two inches away from my ankles, I did not show anything off, I already had considered that. But no, I looked like a whore. He ripped the 40 dress off me. It was ruined. But so was L I Was a positive person trying to do the best in my life. I was a nothing, no one, I was worthless, nasty, ugly, dirty horrible person.

Right, I had it in my head I was leaving Peter. No, I was going to tell him to get out. I started on the pill. I realized it would never be fair to have a baby living like this. But in April I had a test at the doctors and I was pregnant. I knew in my heart I was not going to get rid of it, never again. I was not bothered what Peter said. I remember thinking at the time, it's supposed to be a happy occasion, but not for me. When the doctor told me I was pregnant, I thought, "Oh my God, what was I going to tell Peter?" I knew I was not going through what I did before for him, but I just had to decide how I was going to tell him, and when.

I think a week went past and I just came out with it. I was not bothered what he had to say, I came straight out with it and said I'm not getting rid of my baby again for you. You can leave me if you want, I do not care I'm keeping my baby this time. I could not believe it when I told him straight! HOORAY! I felt like having a victory dance.

But I did pay for it, He said he could not believe he was having a kid with me, he felt so sorry for the baby having a mum like me. No way, he felt embarrassed already. Why couldn't this be a happy occasion with me?

Peter started to hit me only on my head because of the bruises, He would kick me on my head, he did not care how much he hurt me. Throughout my pregnancy he would scream at me and hit me on my head, kicking or with his fist. 41 I used to watch men pushing their kids in the street. Why did it have to be this hard for me?

I used to watch men pushing their kids in the street. Why did it have to be this hard for me? It used to make me upset. Peter did not come with me to scans or anything. I felt like he was trying to ignore it and hoping it was not for real.

The first time Jordan moved in my stomach was when Peter was shouting at me. I would have loved to be happy about it, but nothing in my life made happy. I was controlled 24/7.

I did not go out, only to my Mum's and now and then around to my friend's. I later found out she was going with Peter too behind my back.

During the summer, it was lovely and warm, but only got to look out of the window. Peter would be out all day in the summer time. I would sit there and cry wishing he cared for me and that he would take me out. I would sit there and cry and cry, being lonely is horrible. Then when he did come back in he would shout or hit me when he felt like it. He made me think I'm nothing. I would clean and clean, sometimes to keep busy, and to try to hide the hurt and not think about it, But it never worked. Peter throughout my pregnancy only put his hand on my stomach two or three times, He would keep saying every day and every night how he felt sorry for the baby having a mum like me, I was dirt and scum, I believed what he said was right, it was because of him telling me all the time.

Time went by every day the same day in and day out, I was eight and a half months pregnant. I woke up about 3am in the morning with pain in stomach, Peter had not long come in. I told him that my stomach was hurting, he said it would be OK' and went back to sleep, He was never bothered about me. I will always hate him for that. A few hours went by, I was just walking up and down the living room. I kept going to Peter but he was not bothered. In the end, at about 9am I was trying to walk up the road to the telephone box to phone my friend. I could hardly walk because of the pain.

Peter still didn't believe I was in labor. It took one of his friends who came around who had kids of his own to tell him I was in labor and he should take me to the hospital. So he did. He did not believe me for six hours. His friend came around for five minutes and he believed him. It was not fair.

It was a Saturday morning. Peter took me to hospital and I was nine inches dilated. I had to have my waters broken by a nurse.

I had a baby boy. He was beautiful. Peter was not there at the time as he kept going in and out for a fag. He always wanted a baby girl. He made me feel like I had let him down. He did not stay long after the birth. How sad, he was on me all the time.

Most of the day went past, everyone had their husbands or family around them in other beds. I was sitting all day on my own. Around about 5pm Peter had brought my Mum and his Stepmom. Peter brought me some flowers. It was nice to see a face I knew when my Mum walked in. It made me really happy. I did feel guilty as I did not ring her when I was panicking that morning. I always did after that, I really don't why I didn't. She should have been the first person I rang. If I hurt my Mum that day I really did not mean too. Sorry to my Mum.

We were all talking about names - I could not name my own son. Peter said my name was a silly one (Ryan) because somebody I knew just had a baby boy and named him Ryan. Then I said what about Marcus? Peter said no. Peter's Stepmom said Jordan and I said yes that's a nice name so we all agree my baby son was named Jordan. His second name Marcus.

My son was beautiful and still is, He was a happy baby. Despite everything I was going through, h still had a smile on his face. The day I brought my son home I was so proud. I could not stop looking at him. He was my newborn baby son, WOW! I knew I would love him like a mother should and protect him with my life. I never knew how to hold him at first, I thought I would hurt him. I think it took me half an hour to change his nappy the first time. He was so small, I had no experience with babies. I knew how to love, and that one of the most important things in life is love. I knew how to show it, but it had been a long time since I did because of Peter. It was time to take my son home for the first time, Peter came to pick us up. He brought a newborn suit, top with the bottoms. But it was too big for him. How little his feet and hands were. He was just so beautiful! That was only because he got his looks from me, ah ah!

I sat in the back of the car and did not take my eyes off him. We pulled up slowly into the car park next to where we lived. It was amazing, thousands of cats, everywhere, both of the greens next to where we lived, all of the flats roofs in front of us and across the road, they were everywhere. They had come to welcome Jordan, I got out of the car and me and Peter 1 were just looking at them all, they were all looking at us. But not one moved, as I can remember, or made a noise, It was amazing. Still to this day I remember that moment. But the funny thing was, as soon as we got into the flat, we both looked out of the window and all the cats had gone, Was it a good sign? A bad sign? I never knew. But I had seen these cats before when I was younger. I knew I had seen them before, but don't know how old I was, or when, I still try to think to this day. I will never understand why I saw those cats. I wonder till this day about those cats.

Peter didn't stay in long with me before he went around the pub. A good excuse to have a drink, he said to wet the baby's head. But he was just full of it shit, that is! I never went out for a month, then when I felt I could go out with Jordan I did. But four weeks was a long time, and I was very protective. Peter would say I'm doing everything wrong with him, but I soon learnt. The first two weeks with Jordan went well. But when I took him to bed, every noise I heard I was in there like a shot. I had to make sure my baby was OK. Me and Peter would even argue about it. He said I was too soft with him, he said I should not run in to him every time he makes a noise. He may have been right but it was the way he said it to me.

One day he stopped me from going in. Jordan was crying and it was breaking my heart. He was only baby; He was my first baby. But he was my fourth child. My first baby I got to take home, it was Peter's fourth child as well, but he did have four children to take home, He always said he knew best. How do you know you are doing something wrong, when it's the first time doing it? You learn though experience. He had experience with children, I did not. You learn, you have no choice to. Peter would always tell me I was thick. He was very cruel to me. He still hit me and shouted at me.

My son was a happy baby; he would have not been happy if I was doing everything wrong. Like Peter said I was.

Peter took interest in Jordan when he had his friends around, always making out he was a good dad. But the truth is, he did what he wanted when he wanted. He did not care for us, his woman was always more important to him than myself and Jordan. Peter would always smoke in the same room as Jordan even in the car he would smoke. He said, "It did me no harm." It always had to be his way, his way was the best you see, to him anyway.

Jordan was taken into hospital with a bad chest. I was worried sick about my baby. He was only three months old. When Peter came to visit, he would always shout at me, saying it was my fault that Jordan was ill and he's in hospital. He would shout this so loud that all the nurses and everyone could hear. He was not bothered, because he knew best, you see. He would say what he wanted, do what he wanted,

I hated him inside, but also loved him. I would never give up on him. Even though he was very cruel to me.

I got brought up with morals. I thought once you have a child with someone you stay with them through thick and thin, like a marriage. There was only one time I can remember Peter helping me with Jordan.

I woke up, and I could not see Jordan. I jumped up and ran to find Peter. I opened the living door to find Jordan was fed and changed and dressed. Peter did it, I could not believe it. Jordan was sitting on the settee smiling his head off. He looked so cute and beautiful. He was my baby who I loved so much. I thanked Peter for looking after him. He said, "That's OK." My God, it was his own son who I thanked him for. But did not let that bother me, as long as my baby OK I was not bothered.

It was so nice to get a bit of help, those few hours of sleep did me a lot of good. It would have been nice if he did it more often. It would have helped mc so much. Peter would moan to me that we were spending no time together and I would fall asleep so early at night. This was because I did everything for Jordan, feeds every three hours at night, everything. This was the only time I remembered him helping me the first and last time. How could I forget!

My Mum and Stepdad helped me once. It was the night he got taken into hospital. So I did not ask again after that. But if I did everything for my son, at least he was OK and looked after properly.

I can remember when Peter was really shouting at me in the living room. He was upsetting my baby son, who started to cry and I cried because Jordan looked so scared and upset. But Peter was not bothered. He had to have his say, because everything he said was right! I would stand there and listen like I was a little girl being told off for being naughty.

Peter always made me feel so low. worthless. Peter's friends would play with Jordan when they came to visit, it was so nice. Just someone taking an interest in us. Peter's friends could see I looked after Jordan properly. They also knew Peter was unfair to me. They never said it, but I knew it. Moan and moan and moan, Peter would every day. My life was hard enough. But like I said nothing was good enough for Peter. I would never win. I was just hopeless he would say.

I would have loved to have had a loving partner who cared for me and his son. Instead of going out with his brother with girls or his friends with girls. Having a good time was more important than me and his son. Why? That was not normal, was it? Or is it me again?

CHAPTER 4

My heart ached enough, I had had enough! GOOD BYE PETER.

He went out every night, I'm always on my own. It was not fair on me. What had I done to deserve this? God, please help me.

So one day I'd had enough. Peter came home in the early hours as usual. I got up 6am one morning, packed all I could and phoned a taxi down to my Mum's. Me and Jordan were off— SEE YA!

Peter was just a lump of horse poo, a useless man. It's not fair, he's just a false person, he gave me false hope. I soon realized, but got in too deep. As I began to think about running off, actually doing it, it was amazing, cool! FREEDOM!

I thought wrong.

God, why has my life always been so hard? I didn't want to give up. I had my son to think of, and I wanted to be the best mum in the world. I begged God to help me get stronger, I needed to be, but I found it so hard. Three years I was with Peter in the flat. I let him on my tenancy, well did not have a choice really. I never had a choice, my life was not his, he told me what do and when do it. NO NO NO NO MORE!

I got everything I needed anyway and went like the wind. In this taxi, I asked the taxi driver to "step on it!" I thought it was funny. I had always wanted to say that. I kept laughing through being so nervous.

I got in that taxi with my son Jordan, as fast as I could. I kept dropping things, because I was right outside the flat. Peter snoring away in cloud 9 and me running around like mad, because of panicking so much. It was a good job I put Jordan in the taxi. I might have forgotten him and left him on the footpath outside my flat I was running away from. Anyway, that did not happen, thank you God. It's funny now to think of it. But anyway, there I was sitting in the back of a taxi with Jordan. There was hardly any space at all, but if could have put the kitchen sink in the taxi, I would have done.

I arrived at my Mum's, knocking like mad, begging her to open the door because I had run off from Peter. I was so, so scared, too, but got everything out of the taxi, paid the taxi driver and made a lot of mess in my Mum's hallway. I really had no choice, but I knew my Mum would have helped me if she could. Thank you Mum xxxx.

Every day Peter would hit me, he had punched my head, kicked my head, I could not take any more. I wanted more for my son, not this life. I so wanted a normal household, for my son to have a Mum and a Dad. Why this had to happen to me please, why? I used to cry when I was out and see Dads pushing their baby or child, why didn't me and Jordan deserve this?

I dropped everything off and went to my friend's, thanking my Mum because she let me leave my stuff there. 1 went to my friend's flat, but at the time 1 did not realize she had already been with Peter behind my back. How sick, i thought she was my best friend, she was just.

It was marathon day. Each year the North staffs run though my estate, which at the time when 1 told the taxi driver "step on it" i did not realize it was that day when Peter realized I was gone he could not do anything because all the roads were blocked off, haha!

I had to go the local council and apply for another place to live.

Me and my son Jordan had to stay with my friend for about three weeks and then the council offered me a three-bedroomed house. It was on the same estate. I was very excited. This was a new start for my son and me.

But Peter knew all along where we were, through my friend. They had been seeing each other all along. How can you do that to someone and look at them in the face?

When Peter knocked on my friend's door, I didn't know what to say. I was very scared. Jordan, my darling son, was nine months old. He was just playing and did not realize the horrors of life. He was a happy baby, which always kept my strength up. I tried so hard to be a good Mum. My son deserved so much in life. I wanted to show my son how to be strong in life and I used to tell him, "life is only what you make it", but in fact that was not the case for me. Every time I tried to do well in life Peter would destroy it. Peter had a lot of friends. Friends who would tell him if they had seen me and who with. I was always getting watched. I was not doing anything wrong, so I did not worry about anything. But it was different for Peter. he had a number of girls he used to see and at the time still did. He was hitting me, hit me, kick me, punch me all the time and for what? It was because he was doing it behind my back. I got treated the way I did because he was seeing girls, He would treat the girls so well, but he took me for granted, Peter would say if only I had a little girl, he would have treated me better. How on earth is that my fault? Why do I always get the blame?

After staying with my friend Sharon for a few weeks, me and Peter were getting on great. He played with Jordan he came to see us. It so nice. I had never really seen him care for our son the way he did then. He showed so much love and care devotion to him. It was a lovely picture. We both agreed got on better without living together.

My new home was only up the road from here, not far I told Peter and I was very excited. A new start, a good start I hoped and wished for.

I think about the house and life I would have liked would have loved to have. But it never came true, the memories from the house are sad ones. Lonely ones, sad ones, so much pain and heartache. This is all I knew. The only adult life I had experienced.

There was no love to be seen, but there was so much love to give. But if there \vas no love there, what was I trying to grab on to? If there was no love, then why do I keep holding on? I was trying to grab at something that was not there, but always hoped for.

FREEDOM was not that easy to find, to hold on to, it was too far for me to reach. I tried so much to grab it, but it kept letting go of me. People can take their lives for granted, but for me life was an imprisonment, upset and hurt. Keeping my faith was all I had. If you can help yourself in life and be positive, this can save your life. By being positive you can make more positive things happen. But what happens when all your faith has been beaten out of you? What do you do? Where do you go in your own mind? What can help you now? Who can help you now? God? I needed a miracle.

If but being positive could help you in many ways. everyone in life tries to be positive, this world would be a better place because life is hard enough to live. Think of three positive things you can do in one day. Just by brushing your teeth once a day, or doing your nail polish and making sure your nails look nice every clay, and even doing your hair each day could make a lot of difference to you. It Was three positive things you did not do the day before. So WELL DONE to you. Anything is better than nothing. you need to believe in yourself and let faith give a helping hand.

Life, do you hope to happen, and what happens are two different things. Your beliefs and your heart and your sense of believing have vanished into thin air. Nowhere to be seen and unable to reach. But if you have dreams in life, please never give up on them. Dreams have to start from somewhere. If you truly believe it's in the far distance, one day you will be able to reach it. Please don't give up, you need to reach out and believe it, it can help you with your hope and faith. DO IT AND WANT IT. Dreams are never to be forgotten. Faith can be in many shapes and sizes. It doesn't matter how big or small, just remember dreams have to start from somewhere, and yes even your own. From the moment I moved in to the house, until the day I left it, freedom was nowhere to be seen. Love didn't show itself for a long time. The reason there was none was because he was being unfaithful to me, but saying I was. My life was also serious because they know what they are doing, but they won't admit it and will blame you for all the downfalls in life, because he will not except he is in the wrong. By then, it was not the first time he two-timed me and it was not the last. It does not matter what you do for them, nothing will ever be good enough.

CHAPTER 5

A new start

B ut yet three years on, Peter was still hitting shouting at me and making sure all signs of happiness had gone away, and making sure he took piece of my heart each time.

But one thing he did do right is make sure myself and Jordan always had enough money. But that was until his girlfriend who moved in with him found out. Then he stopped all money. The money was for his son to make sure he had everything he needed, so giving me and his son a bit extra each week would have not made a difference to him, but no, his girlfriend's always came first, even before his own son.

The past few months before I left the flat, I was saving money. I called it 'my run away money'. I needed to make sure I had enough money for myself and my son, well my son mainly. I did not want my son to go without, because I ran away from his Dad. I wanted to try to build a life where he was happy, and got everything he needed in life. He was only nine months old when we ran away.

I used the money to get my kitchen stuff, my fridge, washing machine and cooker, everything was secondhand, but everything worked and lasted for three years or more. I can remember getting a hew high chair for Jordan. God, he was my beautiful and funny son. Things (food) may have landed on the walls and all over his face and then he would play his feet, so yes he used to get covered in what he eating. It so funny.

I also brought Jordan a car, one he could sit in and go around by himself on, but he was too small for it at first and his foot did not touch the pedals. But after a few months he was going around the garden 40mph. Ah, he loved it so much, and I loved it when he happy. If it was not for my son, I don't think I be here today. you have got to be strong for our kids, unless how are they going to learn how to be strong in life? You as a parent have a very big role in your children's life, you are their main teacher in life. I tried to start a good circle of hope for my son. It was very hard but you need to try your best and do it for your children and teach them that abusing your partner is in no way right. Love, trust and honesty is needed in everyone's life.

After I got everything for my new home, I felt proud of myself. Jordan was looked after and my house was looking pretty good. I loved it. This was a new start. -My new start. I made the rules in this house and my God it felt so strange. I forgot what it was like making my own decisions. I felt it hard. But I had to get on with it, I was being watched everywhere I went. Peter said I was. But that did not bother me. As I only cared for my son. NOT another man. He was trying to scare me, but I had nothing to worry about as I was not doing anything wrong.

Soon it was summer, I got Jordan a slide, a swimming pool mini one), a go-kart, well lots of things I got for him to play in the garden with. The car I brought him, well he aced that now. "Go Jordan!" He learnt how to use the pedals properly and off he went. I would have to chase him around, he would not stop laughing and then he would suddenly stop and then carry on pedaling for his life. Speedy should have been his nickname'. I loved playing with my son in the garden. He was my life and still is, but that is something he will come to learn as he has his own children.

Peter hardly came to visit us over the summer. It was very hard for me; I was so lonely. Once Jordan in bed I would cry my eyes out, because all I wanted was to have a family and be with a man that loved us both and did actually spend time with us. How can you ignore your children? All because he wanted to have a good time with other women and drink a lot. I had to think, has this man got a heart? NO. Did he care for us? NO. To all questions, the answer would be NO.

He used to come to visit us once a month. Jordan would be in bed by the time he would come. I really felt honored for him to come. I really did. I loved him so much. I just wanted him to love me back, and his son of course. I would think why only once a month? I try to make each visit better than the last time because I believed I was not making him happy. So I tried everything in my power to try to make him care for us. I believed it was all my fault. He made me think I was not good enough for him and I should be lucky he comes at all.

He would stay the night and leave early in the morning. When he left I would cry my eyes out for three days solid. I knew it would be a few weeks till I saw him again. Why don't I deserve to be happy? What have I done to deserve this? I would pray to God to be happy one day and Jordan would have a dad who cared and took more time out to be with us.

CHAPTER 6

The truth

After walking back my mums one day, I saw a dear friend of mine (Katie) who told me the truth. It the reason why Peter only came once a month. It was his girlfriend's period time of the month I could not believe this. Katie told me that she (Peter's girlfriend) was going to have Peter's baby. This hurt me so much, He lived with another girl and another girl who was only 17 years old at the time was having his baby. I felt like my life was over, so I found where he was. He was having a drink with her and his friends in the local pub. So that is where I wanted to hurt her so much. But it was all Peter's fault. I looked through the window of the pub and then ran in.

I shouted: "Where is your girlfriend, then Peter? I thought I was your girlfriend? But no, you've got another at your flat too."

I made sure everyone could hear me. Peter could not believe his eyes and ears. I did not tell him how I found out but made sure I called her a lot of names before Peter ordered me out of the pub.

He said, "I'm going to beat you for this! You made me look a fool."

"That's because you are a fool," I shouted. "what about me and Jordan? why are we not good enough to be in your life?"

He could see how hurt I was but still warned me to go home or else. So I walked off crying. This was painful to me, but Peter did not care. Then I became scared because he said made him look a fool. Then I cried, then was scared and cried over and over. I did not look forward to him coining to see me next.

I should have been used to Peter having other but it still hurt me so much, each time and each girl I told about. When is enough is enough? Why did I give my heart to someone that didn't really care? But the arguments and beating I was told 1 was loved otherwise he would not bother.

So I should be happy? What a strange way. But it's their way. They have suffered, so they are not willing to give their hearts away again. So they make you suffer, because of something that happened to them.

After being told about Peter and his other girlfriend, I just to forget about it. This girl was fully aware about me and Jordan, but still carried on with Peter like I did not care. Was I invisible? Was that it? All my life felt like a dream. I'm just waiting and to wake up.

Over the summer Peter did come a few times to take me and Jordan to my Mum's. I would see a girl's coat in the car and girl's shoes in the car. I just got told "Don't touch them!" Like it was normal for me to see this. Peter is so heartless and selfish through and through.

The night I found out about Peter I cried my heart out; that night and every night from then on. I cry and cry.

Peter was so cruel. He had taken a big part of my heart and soul. I was so tired and sick of these games I just wanted to get on with my life. Without all the is at my heart's expense.

I wanted Jordan to have parents that got on. Not argue every day. I didn't want him to hear me screaming or crying. All because of Peter, yet again. all because of his temper, I had to suffer. I did not want Jordan to be like this. He was my son and too beautiful to hurt me like his Dad. My son will never end up like that. I would make sure of this and try to be the best Mum in the world. I wanted my son to be happy in life. He will never go without, not without food or clothes or love. Everybody needs to be shown love is good for you. But show too much to the wrong person and it can bite you in the bum. Love is a very powerful subject, why abuse someone's love? Love is special, ONLY give your love to someone that loves you back and you KNOW they love you, please. You treat each other like an equal.

I could not get the idea of running off out of my head. It was a little seed that grew and now it started to grow more. But this seed is too important to let die. The idea the seed may not grow long or much at all because it is not the right time to run off etc. But this seed needs faith to grow. You know it's there and some day it will grow more, when your faith is ready. At the right time and place, hopefully one day. Yes, believing is seeing, but you've got to believe in it to see it.

I knew deep down I wanted to run off with Jordan because I wanted to save his life from his evil Dad. He was using my son against me, like it was normal to tell him "ignore your Mum". If I was going to run off with Jordan it had be the perfect plan, otherwise I was dead meat.

I wanted to start a good circle of hope. For Jordan. My son deserves this. The men in Peter's side of the family have always treated their like this. I wanted to break the chain. "There is no way my son will turn out like this. I try my hardest to b good mum.

There were times over the summer holidays that Peter would come in a bad mood and he would argue with me. There was always something he shout at me about. There was always something to moan about me, he would say. Nothing was ever good enough for him. My life was so hard to live. Just to get through a day was a challenge, day in and day out, is a survival for your life. I never knew what would happen next. What I would get the blame for again, everything was always my fault. Peter would start an argument if there was a dog hair on the sponge, nothing was ever up to his standard. Then I would be kicked down to the floor because of the dog hair. A few times this happened to me. Peter would always pick a fault. He must be called Sir Idiot Man or Girlie Pants!

I used to love the times he popped in, hit me, then go again, all in 10 minutes. I'm so lucky!

Love was a joke, Peter is a joke, life was a big joke on me. Please help me God.

Every night the same pattern, cry and cry and cry till all my tears ran out, I felt so empty. Why me? Why can't I be happy? Don't I deserve to be happy? I try my best every day, I do the best I can, but it's never good enough. I do so much to make him happy, so he won't hit me. But he does it anyway. I love him and I hate him, I can't win. What am I going to do?

My heart and my faith was like, please God, why me? I can't take this anymore. Please help me God!' I'm sick of living a life like I'm nothing. Please help me feel strong enough and have faith and believe I be out of here one day I can never give up this dream. I just can't.

Every morning I woke up, I just dreaded it, it the same old day. Just me and Jordan. it was mentally hurting me. But it didn't matter what happened in life for me, I had to make an effort for my son.

I needed to make my son be strong enough in life so he didn't have to suffer things in life such as domestic violence, or drugs, like his Dad. I needed to make him strong enough to never give up in life. My son so deserved a good life. I had to show him he can have a good life. But I wasn't sure how I was going to show him, but I had to. It was my job as his Mum.

Every morning I felt like my heart was ripped out. I had a baby to look after and to try to save myself every day. Life was so hard. I would start the day off being miserable, which did not help me. I would miss Peter so much. I could never stop thinking of him. I could not help it. How was I going to change this? I had to, and to try to save my son.

My son was the most important thing in my life, I would do anything to make him happy and not to worry about anything in life. There are always things in life you don't want to happen. You have to fight and make sure it will be OK, to a level anyway.

I think I lived in dream land. It was the circle of hope. I would imagine Peter asking me to marry me and saying sorry for his affairs and live happily ever after. The circle of hope can be very strong to break. But if you close your eyes and imagine, dreams can come true. If you can imagine it then it can happen. But finding the way is so, so hard.

Anyway, I would get up and give Jordan his breakfast and have a cuppa and a fag. I would be so miserable. After sitting there and crying for a few hours I would let Jordan go and play in the garden. It would be 9am Sunday morning. I used to wake up with Jordan every morning at 6am.

It was 9am and the sun was shining and my son was playing in the garden. Going around in his car, making all the noises a car can make. with a beep beep! It was so funny, I loved to watch Jordan play and enjoy himself. He has no worries except to play in the garden with his toys when he can. I will never forget those days with Jordan. I watched him from the moment he could not walk or talk and now he's my little man. The days were very hard but I had to get on with it and be strong for my son. Well the best way I could anyway.

CHAPTER 7

My life

When Jordan went to bed, I would want to scream at the top of my voice, and do anything to try get this upset ness out of me. I would sit there and wonder what Peter was doing. Which girl he was with tonight. Why could he not love me enough to stay more than he did. Why couldn't my son have a Dad in his life a lot more. You think why, why, why?

I tried to start a life which I wanted to live in. So I started with the things around me first. The garden was not that nice. Lots of big bricks and mud, and I wanted to try to get it looking nice. Jordan played in the back garden and at the side. I wanted to try to do more and be positive. Also to try to get the front garden to look nice. I decided there and then that day, what needed to be done first. There were lots of big bricks so I got rid of them first, and the rubbish too. I went through it all on a nice summers day, which I loved doing. I enjoyed gardening and so did my Mum. It's time out and you can think better. Well sometimes anyway!

At the side of the house there was a gate. But there were gaps each side of the gate where it not been done properly. So my darling beautiful son would decide to try to pass me and run out of the gate, which he thought was very clever, laughing while he did it. I would be gardening and suddenly I will think it's gone very quiet, so I would look for Jordan in the back garden and he was not there. Then I would run out of the garden to see his little legs run for his life while he was laughing because now he knows I'm chasing him. He would look back and laugh so much and run off again.

When I was close to him, I would slow down then stop. To try to get him to think I'm tired. He would then be looking around at me, at that point I used to jump up and run for my life after him. At 0.01 mph ahhh! I would not leave it too long around the block. So that's when I turned in to an ugly monster which was going to eat him alive well, pretending was so funny. Anyway I pretended to be a monster and he would be laughing his little head off because he didn't realise I was only trying to get him back in the garden. But I would try not to panic, because I realised I'd left my front door open. "Oh my God" was going around in my head. So I was the ugly monster who picked him up on my shoulders to take him back to my castle to make a nice stew out of this beautiful little boy who will get sent to bed if he decided to do it again!

A few times I would be doing the front garden and I would just jump up automatically and run for my life around the block for Jordan, and without checking in the garden first. So when I got back to the house, I would get back, to find him in the back garden • Jordan would be wondering why my face was so red and wonder why I could not catch my breath for dear life, after chasing fresh air. At least my son was OK that was all that matters. Thank you God XXXX.

Stef, my twin sister, only came round when she wanted something. One day she knocked on me door. I was not going to answer, but I did. She said she was pregnant. She was three months. I could see by her stomach that she was not lying. I still did not believe her 100% until she was getting bigger in the stomach area. I started to cook a meal for her each time she came. Looking after my sis, it was nice. But due to the fact she took drugs she had to stop. But she said it was too hard. I really felt sad for her baby because as she was on drugs, her baby was too.

I did not understand about it all as I never took drugs. But I knew it was not good and I was worried for my niece/nephew. I could not understand. Once she realized she was pregnant, why on earth did she not try get off them? But that was her story and her decision. I would think it was very selfish. But she was not the only woman to do this. Until you have experience of something, you don't know how it feels. But me personally don't understand how you would not come off straight away, but like I said another story.

She tried to do her drugs in front of me a few times, but I could not stand there and see her inject something. It made me feel sick. She always tried to take advantage of my kind nature. She will never change! It's a shame really.

Her baby, my niece, was born, and she was very beautiful. But she had to be weaned off heroin. I could not imagine a baby on that. I thought a lot of people would, but it was very cruel to her. But a lot of woman do this. I never will understand. But Sasha was very beautiful.

She looked like her auntie a lot (me!) only joking. Sasha had to go into intensive care. I helped to feed her. With having a baby, myself I knew how to pick her up and wind her. By then Jordan was one year and three months.

It was not a good time for me, due to Peter spending most of his time with his other girlfriend. It made me feel sick. Peter was a twisted person indeed VI always thought the grass was greener the other Sid but learnt it was black. Hah, in your face! He always came back to me. Peter knew I loved him.

By then, we had been together for three years. Peter had to go jail for three months because of drink. driving and all his girlfriend's went off with other men Some were his friends. I was so gutted for him! Like I said, "in your face!" I felt for him. Well, he acted like an idiot, so serve him right. Shame!

I used to get on with Peter's friends. They knew I used to get on with Peter's friends. They knew Peter was being sad on me. But I had to be careful when talking to them as Peter would get jealous, and then he would beat me up after for it. So I did not ignore them, but did not go out of my way to make a conversation with them. I would be talking to them and as soon as Peter walked back in the room, I went back to being a little mouse. His friends realised why I did this, which I thought was so funny. They were supposed to be on his side but felt like they felt sorry for me and knew I was a good person. But they carried on with the act. I did not feel they were his true friends, but if I said that to Peter he would wonder why I said it and the reason, which I could not say — that I felt like his friends would try to make me laugh and start talking to me once he left the room.

I would have got the blame for something which was not going on, except conversation. But to Peter he would make a mountain from a mole hill. I used to think "idiot man", thought he knew everything. No one can know everything. There are a lot more things in the world to learn from more knowledge is better. Like I said 'idiot man'.

CHAPTER 8

Peter

Peter really used to upset me. I could talk to anyone except him. He made me feel like I was nothing. He broke my heart and the old confident me was nowhere to be seen. He destroyed me and that was only three to four years into the relationship. What a jolly life I had! I used to feel for my son. Through the summer we hardly went anywhere. I looked after lot my son 24/7. Peter was well too busy having fun and spending all his money. I loved looking after my son, but it was hard yes. Most days once I got over the mornings I would be OK, to a point anyway. God he Jordan made me laugh so much. Peter was losing so much time with our son, which would have been good for him, but no not Peter. He told me he did not have a good relationship with his father so he could have changed the pattern but he decided like his father before him, to go out and have fun with different woman and drink all the time.

I started to go to my Mum's nearly every day. One day, Jordan's water from warming up his bottle went on the settee. The thing was it was my Mum's new settee and even though it would have been OK by just giving it a wipe, my Mum decided to kick off I found myself in the kitchen while she was trying to strangle me. She was acting like she wanted to kill me and it really hurt me. I could not believe it. I would never fight my Mum back so I put my hands on her shoulders and locked my arms straight so she could not get to me. All the time I was watching my Mum pull these nasty faces and really gritting her teeth. I really thought she hated me.

My Mum did not realize what I was going though at the time with Peter. But every time I went I used to buy them a cake etc., from the bake shop across the road. I really used to enjoy doing things like that for them. It was something simple but I enjoyed it. When I used to knock on the door, my Slum would answer the door and I would say "Hi Mother dude" and give her a hug. My mum would always smile when I said that, so I did it every time to make sure I made her smile at least once that day.

I loved my Mum very much. But due to her drinking and the love she had for my Dad, it ruined her. My Mum never got over my real Dad. Even my Stepfather realized this and they had been married nearly 15 years. And all of us knew she still loved my real Dad because she would never let us forget. She would shout it out even then after 15 years. She would still shout "I love you Desmond Beach". At this point my Stepdad should have been used to my Mum when drinking. She could be quite nasty. She never excepted the fact that she broke up with my Dad and would not still to her dying breath. My Mum unhappy for years. Drink was the only thing she had to escape.

Escape from life, and such a jolly life it was! Not really, when you suffer domestic violence in your life. When you are the one who is getting hurt. You are hurt because they are beating you up. But because you have done nothing wrong. You never understand how someone you love hurts you like that. You think' why? When you love someone and they hurt you. It hurts more because you love them. The circle of hope has started and it's not that easy to get out of.

When my Dad died my Mum used to shout that she wanted to be dead with my Father. My Dad died when I was nine years old. She would also shout it in front of my Stepfather. I did used to feel sorry for my Stepfather. He loved her so much. But the trouble was she loved someone else too much. Yes, my Mum did care for Stepfather, but she soon wished it was my real Dad instead. The thing was he knew it too, which I did think was cruel for him. I do think he realized I knew it because I liked to help a lot.

I used to water her Q.C sherry down. Like I told you near the beginning of my story, I never stopped loving my Mum for one second. But what there was here was an issue domestic violence is the issue. Even when the person is not in your life, you can still feel the hurt. You can never get rid of the heartache in your mind. In your mind it will always stay, but some people can push it back more than others. None of the violence was necessary, so why? To make themselves feel better!

When you are sitting on the floor like a dog, because you dare not get up, at the time you are scared. You sit there and think what just happened and you think "why me?" and cry and it hurts so much more and you cry and hurt more. No one has the right to do this, I want everyone to realize about the issue. It has been around for years and it will still in years to come. It should be in peoples' lives, the upset and hurt, and people should realize more about this issue because it could help to save lives. So this issue should not be hidden, but in public view.

Peter hardly came around because he was so busy with his girlfriend and their baby. They had a little boy called Hayden. I so laughed because Peter so wanted a little girl. He now had five boys. Ah, in your face! My baby, Jordan's brother or sister, was buried at five months, I do believe was a girl. I was told by a tarot reader. I was told they named my baby Emily in heaven, and that she looked happy and was there waiting for me. She was with a lady that sounded like my Mum. It still rips my heart out and always will. LOVE YOU MY DARLING.

I was never allowed to talk about my baby. Not allowed to show emotion. I was like a robot. I never realized until writing my story that I never went to my baby's funeral. I never asked. I can't believe it. I did not even think to ask. When I gave birth to my baby I never looked but squeezed my eyes shut. I gave names for both male/female. I was sad and I'm so sorry to my baby and to God. Please forgive me.

I live out the pain still to this day. There is not a day goes by where I do not cry. PLEASE don't put yourself through this pain. Think ahead for your future, with your head and heart please. If I can help you not to go through the same pain as me, it would be amazing to yourself and your heart.

CHAPTER 9

Why Peter?

One day when Peter came to visit. I lost it. I was NOT bothered what he did to me. He could not hurt me more than he already had.

I told him, "Go away! Go to your new baby and your tart of a girlfriend. I never will forgive you. You heartless person."

I could not stop shouting at him. It was in front of the whole street. I let it out and called him every name I could while I could! He did not shout back at me, which I was surprised at, but did not care anyway. He could see how hurt I was. But because he could see I was so hurt he took Jordan away from me to hurt me more. He said he was told I was seeing someone, so I had to pay for it and also because I shouted at him. Peter knew he had lost me, so he took Jordan and came back after to beat me up.

But as soon as I heard his car again I stopped crying and grabbed the keys to my house and ran for my life. Well tried to. He saw me open the door to run, so shut the door quick and ran through the house to the back door. He thought I was still in the house. I ran into next door's garden. He knew I could not be far as he had all ways covered by his friends. My heart was beating 100mph. It felt like I could hear the beats, I was so scared and out of breath. I had to hold my breath and to calm my breathing down in case he heard me. He started to shout my name and warned me if I did not come out of the corner I was hiding in, I would be sorry. But I did not move. He thought would be too scared and come out from where I was. My beautiful son had just been kidnapped from me and I could not stop thinking about Jordan. I Stayed in the bushes for a little while till everyone went. I thought about the spiders and webs in the bushes, I had seen the day before when putting out the washing— the spiders were quite big and I was sitting there with them. Awwvv!

When I thought I was safe, I jumped up. But peter was waiting for me because he knew I could not be far. I put the key in the door and he was calling me a few names. "SHI T," I thought and ran for my life again, but I ran around the block into the garden behind my next-door neighbor's and did a U-turn straight in my back door. Peter saw me run down the road. But he did not think I would dare to sneak back in the

house under his nose. I hid under the kitchen table for a few hours, just in case. I ended up crying my eyes out all night and lying under Jordan's cot. I slept with his cover and his favorite toy, praying for my son to be given back. But I realized it was not going to be easy for me. Nothing with Peter was easy. I hate him. He's an "idiot of a man" and very heartless. But he took my son just to hurt me and get me back because I told him I hated him etc. He realized I really meant what I said.

The next day I woke up, it was Christmas Eve. I just cried my eyes out. I had bought Jordan a bouncy castle with a ball pit. God, it took so long to blow it up. I also got him a drum and guitar set. I knew he would drive me crazy with it, but he was not here to open his presents. I brought him so much and it took me all year to pay for them. I was more excited for him for Christmas morning. Peter always ripped my heart out, I did not realize how cruel he was and to what depths he'd go to hurt me.

I did not know what to do. Sly head and my heart was hurting so bad. It felt like my heart was going to jump out. I could not cry any more. All my tears had run dry. I went to a friend's then went to my Mum's. I wanted to tell my Mum how sorry I was and to tell her what happened. I could not stop crying. But she also knew I could not stay long because Peter might come. I did not want to leave but I had to, because I did not want to cause any trouble for my Mum and Stepdad. Sly Mum knew how scared I was but still told my Stepdad to give me a lift. I was so scared to walk in the street. It was so nice of my Mum. She knew I did not want to cause any trouble for her, but she still wanted to try to protect and help me if she could. I got in the car but lay down. I was so thankful to my Mum. She did make me laugh when I said I did not want a lift because I did not want to cause any trouble for them. She said, "No, we will help you and give you a lift. You are my daughter I love so much."

I had tears in my eyes and I gave my Mum a great big hug. I will never forget it. I told my Mum how much I missed her and loved her before I left.

When I got back to my house I did not turn the lights on at first. It was Christmas Eve and I was so lonely. Thinking of my son and if he was here when he woke up in the morning to see his presents from me. Peter took that treasured moment away from me. As he took everything which was good in my life from me.

It was Christmas morning and I just woke up and cried. why does my life have to be so hard? 1 down to my friends and tried to enjoy the day the best way I could. Boxing day about tea time I went to see my Slum and Stepdad. I wanted to let them know I was OK so they did not too much about me. I can remember talking to my Mum and it was lovely.

My Slum said sorry to me for over the years, and even though I was the strongest I still needed the love. She said sorry with tears in her eyes. She said, "I did not realize how strong you are and I'm very proud of you. I'm so sorry I have not shown it to you. I you, very much. I'm so sorry my beautiful daughter."

I said to my Slum, "I'm only beautiful because I look like you."

She smiled and I give her a big fat hug. I knew my Mum meant what she said, it was very deep what she said to me. I knew she meant it because she had never done that before and it felt amazing.

The relationship I always wanted with my Mum. I really felt happy with my Slum and I could see she felt happier for saying it too. It was super, super cool. That night I don't think I moved from my Mum's side. I did not want to leave the house because I felt that happy with my Mum. My Slum was so funny when n she swore. It was so funny. I said, "Mum, I love you and you are super cool. I hope you know that."

I thought at that moment how much I loved he r.

I never asked for anything when I moved out properly at 18 years old with Peter. Stef asked for money every day. My sister lived with them at that point I think. Well, do you know what, I can't remember if she lived with my parents or not! Anyway, my Mum and Stepdad adopted Sasha, Stef's daughter.

I have the last few photos of my Mum with Sasha, a week before Mum died. My mum looked very tired and not too well in the photos. Her eyes looked d deep and hurt still. All that time, I was not talking to Mum. I liked to think I tried to cheer my mum up. But she was used to doing this. it wasn't until I not talking to her she realized how much effort I used to make when I came to visit. But I do agree, in went down too much. But just did not realize it at the time. I took my parents for granted, that's why I went every day. But everybody needs time to themselves. I realized some things too. I asked my mum if I could use her phone to ask peter about having Jordan back.

He just swore a lot and put the phone down. I was so upset and my Mum could see I was so she phoned Peter herself. He swore at my Mum too and it was unforgiveable. I hated him even more at that point but could not say anything back to him unless he stopped me seeing my son again.

I said to my Mum a hundred times "Sorry, sorry, sorry" because of Peter. I think my Mum realized even more what an idiot of a man Peter was and how cruel he was. I left my Mum's that night feeling a lot better for talking to her and it was lovely what she said to me and I will never forget that Boxing Day with my Mum.

Two days after, Peter said he felt guilty for the way he spoke to me and my Mum over the phone and he brought back the angel of my eye. My beautiful darling son. God J cried and Jordan was just looking at me. He looked like he had got bigger. Ile had a new tracksuit on -green and white. Ile looked like a cool dude! He did not come to me at first. Ile looked confused and J think he was not sure what his dad was going to say, because he kept turning his head back to his Dad. Peter said to Jordan, "Go on, go to vour Mum." He ran towards me and I hugged him and I think I nearly squeezed him to death. I let go after a bit and went into the house. I told Jordan about his presents from me and there he was the little angel playing on the drums at 8pm at night. I was not bothered; it was pure bliss for him to drive me crazy with the noise he made. He played on the drums and I played on the guitar. We made a right pair! You could hear we were not too great on the instruments but we did not care bang bang and a doff doff from me on the guitar. We thought we sounded great. We had fun and did not care what the neighbors thought.

I will always treasure that moment, it was great. I could not wait to tell my Mum. She would be so happy. Knowing Peter brought Jordan back to me. It was because of my Mum helping me by phoning Peter that he gave Jordan back. I could not wait to tell her. What makes me upset is that I could hardly go out, with not talking to my parents for a year, I just stayed in a lot. It was the last week my Slum was alive and because it was really hard for me to get ready and go out of the door I missed seeing my Slum for the last time. I always hate myself for that. But I could not help it. It became hard to go out of the door. Pete r was still hitting me and it was not at a good time.

CHAPTER 10

My Mum's Death

One morning I got ready and made it out of the door. I was just walking out of the gate when my sister came with Sakha, asking me if I could just look after her for a few hours. I said yes but if I said no she have taken her to a drug dealer's house and I did not want that for my beautiful niece. I could not believe it all that effort just to get to the gate and back again.

But at that point I did not realize my Mum would die in two days' time and that was my very last chance of seeing her. All because I suffered from depression, I spoilt it for myself. Still to this day I think to myself my Mum would not have died if I had been to see her. It was me who used to help my Slum when she was drinking. I would comb her hair and try to do her nails and water down her drink. The most important thing, I thought, was I would always try to get my Mum to feel good about herself and get her to smile. It was important to do that as I would always look in my Mum's eyes and feel her pain because she looked so sad.

I so wished I did not have a problem with being able to go out. I missed the opportunity to see her for the very last time. It was all because of Peter. I HATE YOU 1 HATE YOU 1 HATE YOU. 1 let myself down at a most important time. I will never forgive myself for being so weak. But I could not help it. Sorry Mum!

Stef came back to get Sasha that day and it was too late to go out. For me A night after my Stepdad phoned me in a panic. It was my Mum and she stopped breathing but he had brought her back. He asked me to look after Sasha while he up to the hospital to my Slum. I said of course it was OK. My Stepsister, Sharon, dropped off Sasha. I got her settled with Jordan on the settee where they both OK.

I could not sit down with worry. I phoned Peter in a panic to help me with the kids so I could go up to the hospital to my Mum. Peter came to take me to the hospital with a girl to look after the kids. I got to the hospital and went straight to the emergency department. I said to the nurse my Mother's name and she pointed me to a room to go in where my Stepfather was. I asked to see my Mum and my Stepfather just put his head down. I knew straight away my Mum had died. I just starting crying and hugged my Stepfather. I asked to see my Mum but I couldn't see her. After a little I outside. I sat outside the doors crying my head off. I could not believe it. Sly Mum dead. Nooooooo. It felt like a dream and I wanted to wake up. You don't understand what's going on because you are so upset. I got back home, the girl walked out and Peter went with her. I did not care for them anyway. I sat with Jordan and Sasha.

When I woke up I wished last night was a dream, but I knew I was fooling myself. I tried to play games with my own head so I did not get upset. I had young babies to look after. Sasha was one-year-old and Jordan was nearly two. They woke up being the same little devils they were. They did not know what going on (lucky them). I needed to see my Stepdad regarding Sasha, so I started to get ready to go down to the house.

I did not know what I was going to do because Jordan was still in a pram, too young to walk that far. So I tried carrying Sasha and pushing the pram with one hand. It took me half an hour just to get a little bit down the road. Then there was a beep beep. It was my Stepsister Sharon and her husband. They took Sasha to my Stepdad.

I did not realize my Stepdad was in the police station all night for questioning, regarding my Mother's death. I could not believe it. My Stepdad cared for my Mum so much. But my aunties (my Mum's sisters did not believe him and still think till this day he had something to do with her death. I can't even talk to my aunties about George my Stepdad. They said how well my Mum was doing then BANG she died. They could not believe it or they did not want to believe it because they were hurting.

A week went by and I did not move out of the house. During that week, I had the murder squad at my door regarding my Mum's death. They were asking a lot of questions about my Stepdad. Normally when someone dies they get buried a week after. But due to the police investigation my Mum was not buried till two weeks after.

In between my Mum dying and her funeral, Peter yet again took my son away from me.

He said, "I know you are seeing someone." I could not believe him. I HATED HIM.

My sister Stef came to my house and asked why I not been down to the house. She said Dad thought I did not care for him now because of the police

Investigation. I think I went down that day or the day after. I explained to my sister that I was not being funny at all and to let him know I was OK and I loved him loads and hoped he was OK and to tell him I will be down asap.

When I got down to the house everything was the same except my Slum was not there. It was like she just went out and she'd be back soon well I hoped so) playing games with my head again. I so wanted my Mum to be there.

I went to see my Mum at the mortuary. God the smell of death is not nice. Sly Slum looked beautiful. She had make-up on and just looked like she was asleep. I wanted to shout "wake up!". I went in with my twin sister Stef, but she did not stay long. even argued with my Mum lying there dead. My sister had to start. My Mum's eyes looked a bit open. My sister went to touch her. That is why we argued. But I never got on with my twin sister, she was and is a very selfish person. Still to this day we don't get on and now I'm 38 years old. Anyway Stef went after a little while and I stayed a while longer. It was the last time I was going to see my mum until I go to heaven. I sat on a stool and just looked at my -Mum wondering she had to die, wishing if only I had made an effort to see her, I might be not sitting here now and she would be alive. I will always think "if only", like I said I never will forgive myself for having the problem I had about going out. I wished I could just reverse time just for three or four weeks. I will never ever forgive Peter. Sorry Mum I was not there when you needed me.

I'm not sure it helped not seeing her for a year, but I soon regretted not going down within that year. The things my Mum said to me were lovely. But it was had set its destiny and my died. My Mum so deserved to be happy after all that time. I'm so angry with myself and always will be I should have made that effort, but it was because of Peter beating me up that I hardly went out. I still suffer from it today,

This is why it's so important that I tell my story. For people to read and learn from. Please, please think about my book and don't forget it. Maybe it will save your life one day (hope so) but even if you stop it before the circle of hope starts, it will be YOU that has done it, not me.

I stayed with my Mum for about half an hour at the mortuary, I could not cope with the smell any more. I hoped that my Mum would be OK in heaven and I can remember saying to her that she now had what she wanted all that time to be with my real Dad. I also said I love you, I love you, I love you as many times as I could. I can remember walking out of the room and I walked back in because I did not want to leave my Mum on her own. It was so hard to walk away. But it was her body there and her soul was now with my Dad and I hoped she'd be OK.

I thought about my 5-month-old baby and said to her that she'd be with her too. I still hate myself leaving her on her own. But I could not stay there anymore. I walked out of the main door and took a big breath of the fresh air. Then we ordered a taxi back to my Stepdad. I wanted my Slum to be there and not at the mortuary. Why God, why did this have to happen? Yes, everyone lives and dies but I just wanted a bit more time with my Mum first.

On the day of my Mum's funeral I woke up about 3am in the morning. I did not believe what was ahead that day. I was all on my own. I did not cry, I just sat there and was thinking of my mum. I was telling my Mum how much I loved her and missed her and thank you for saying what she said to me on boxing Day. It was great, well it was amazing and I will never forget that day for as long as I live. I don't know but I could not cry. I so tried but I could not. It was as if my Mum was helping me not to or maybe my Dad was with me too, I don't know but I felt like I was being hugged, but not in a way, But I thanked whoever was helping me.

I got down to my Stepdad's and my sister Stef about 6am in the morning. I stayed in the back garden waiting for a light to go on. I decided to throw bricks at the bedroom window and my Stepdad woke up. So really he did not have a choice! I did not wait that long. But it felt forever. My sister Stef was going on like it was nothing, but my Stepdad could see how much I loved my Mum and I missed her so much already. I said I was very sorry for awaking him. He said he did not mind and gave me a hug.

Before all the family came for the funeral I phoned Peter asking and begging for my son back. He yet again swore at me and called me names and put the phone down on me again. I could not believe his cruel heart.

Well the time came and the limos came to go to the church. Then my Mum was cremated. When I walked out and the cars were there, no one knew who was meant to go first. So I took the lead and got I n the car first before anyone. My aunties were in the car behind. Following my Mum behind the hearse made me feel so sad. I never took my eyes off her. MY Stepdad could see how much I was hurting and held my hand for comfort. But it probably helped him too

When my Mum's ashes were being scattered, some of them went on my top because of the direction of the wind. I kept that top on for at least a week or more. I would have a bath and put it back on without washing it. I could not wash it. Sly Slum was on it. But when I did take it off I still never it and put it in a bag in a special place where no one could get hold of it. I don't know where that black polo neck to. I kept hold of it as long as I could. I thought my Mum would know how much I loved and missed her and always will.

After the funeral we all headed back to my Mum's house. There were drinks and food ready for everyone. As I was sitting there talking to family I hardly knew, I really felt uncomfortable. So I went to sit in the back garden. I was upset about my Mum dying and because Peter would not give me back my son, on a day like this. He was only two years old. He was a cruel-hearted person. I hoped karma got him back for me. I did believe in "what goes around comes around". Karma did get him back, but it was going to take two years. When I escaped with my son Jordan he had nowhere to live and today he is a druggie with no teeth. Ahhh, in your face THANK YOU KARMA.

I did not stay in the back garden long. I spoke with my cousin Jane whilst sitting there. She knew Peter and tried to help me. I thanked her for that. After talking to Jane I went home. I said bye to my Stepdad first then went. It looked like everyone thought it a party, laughing and joking. It made me feel sick so I had to leave.

I walked home very slowly. I could not let today sink in. It was like a dream and I was wondering when I was going to wake up. I can remember getting to the shops near where I lived and seeing an old friend lived two doors up from her as a child. She said she sorry for not going.

I said "it's OK. Your Mum did."

She said she couldn't make it because of her kids, I give her a hug and carried on walking to my house. I must have looked like a lost lamb walking the way 1 did, slowly and with my head down.

Life without my Mum. My life seemed like it was hell. I think life is the hell and heaven is where go for peace when we die. My life has never been good or happy. Thinking about all the people at my Mum's house, it was just wrong. It was NOT a party. They all really upset me. They had hardly anything to do with us all our lives. Then they acted like they all cared which made me feel sick. My Mum used to get upset all my life because her family did not care and hardly ever acted it. They were just false and put on an act for the sake of it. I don't even know what they fell out about. But my Mum and me and Stef suffered because they did not care. We would have loved to have seen our family. I can't ever remember getting a birthday present/card or Christmas present from them at all through my childhood.

When I got home I just sat there, I did not know what to think or how to feel.

The next day I went down to see my Stepdad and Sasha. My sister was there. My Stepdad was happy to see me as he knew I left early the day before. I explained how I felt about it and the family made me feel sick. I said I hardly knew any of my family.

Anyway I got to know my niece a bit more and thought it would have been good if Jordan was here. I went down to my Stepdad's every day for a few weeks, helping him with Sasha. Stef was hardly in. She is a heartless person. Her and Peter would make a good couple.

With my mum gone there \vas a matter regarding the adoption of Sasha. My Stepdad was not well enough to bring her up on his own. Stef I wanted me to move in with our Stepdad to care for Sasha too. I explained I could not because of Peter. I was coping with looking after myself, and the trouble Peter was causing would have not been fair for both Jordan and Sasha. She hated me for that. But it was not me who took drugs through her pregnancy and left everything up to our Mum and Stepdad. She was not allowed to have responsibility for her own daughter. It was not my fault that Sasha went into care.

But she treated me as if it was my fault. One night she said I deserved Peter beating me up. I said she picked drugs over her daughter and that was her fault. I never deserved to be beaten up. We started to fight. I could not believe what she said. She kept asking our Stepdad for money and he was looking after her daughter and she was expecting more still. I hit her like I never had before. I hurt her and won the fight. She ran off crying. I felt bad for hurting her. But all my life she made trouble for me and always she got her own way most of the time. She deserved a slap or two! Karma. I love her, she is great!

Like I said, I was getting to know my niece but she had to go into care because I did not want to move in with them. I felt bad for my Stepdad, but I could not say yes. It would not have been fair for anyone. I wanted to enjoy the time I had with her. It was not for a few weeks. The social worker was due to but with the loss of my Mum they left it a few because they knew I was going down and my Stepsister as too. I would help my Stepdad during the day and then he would get picked up with Sasha to go to Sharon's. They would come back in a few hours. I would sleep there every second night to help with Sasha.

At this point Peter had already had Jordan for three weeks. I kept phoning him to ask him to bring him back to me. But every time the answer would be no. So, I phoned the police for them to help me get Jordan back. The police took me to his flat and I got Jordan back. One of his girlfriends was there. She was swearing and everything. I acted like I was scared of her but I would have loved to have beaten her up. But I had to go by the law if I wanted my son back. So I did.

I got Jordan back and we went straight to my Mum's house. My Mum would have loved it if she could have seen them both playing together. I was happy seeing Jordan. It felt strange having Jordan back. He seemed different. It might have just been me, but it took him a little while to get used to me again too. He started to be really naughty, but that was kids for you. Jordan and Sasha got to know each other for a few weeks.

The day Sasha was due to be picked up to go into care, Stef was there but she left before the social worker came. She did not want to say good bye her daughter. But the thing was she should not have to. She picked drugs over her daughter and now she would have to pay for it. We all had to pay for it. When the social worker came we all just froze and just looked down and tried our hardest not to cry before she left. It was very hard. My Stepdad asked if I could put Sasha in the car. So I picked up Sasha for the last time and started to walk towards the car. The social got in the car and I started to put Sasha in the car. She started to cry and started screaming because none of us were getting in the car with her. I put her in the car seat and strapped her in and give her a last kiss. When I shut the door she was screaming. I had to hold my mouth so I did not cry and the car went off. I watched the car until it went out of sight. When going back in the house we hardly spoke all afternoon. I will never know if I ever will see my niece again. But by law at 18 years she will be told she was adopted.

Still to this day, nearly 17 years on, Stef always blames me for Sasha going into care. It is as if she was the only one who got hurt. Stef Stef Stef! We all had to pay for Stef taking drugs.

I still carried on going down to see Stepdad and slept every second night. He started to go to his daughter's a lot more.

During this period Peter went to jail. Ahh, poor man. What a shame!

CHAPTER 11

Peter's return

When Peter come out of jail, he was on a tag, on his ankle. Also he had to report to the police every morning. I would be writing to him. Telling him how much I loved him still and whatever he did wrong would be forgotten about. He used to write back to me, telling me the same. It was great I felt like it was a new start for us and Jordan have his Dad. I could never give up on him because I wanted my son to have his Dad. It did not matter to me how much pain I went through; it did not matter. As long as my son had his Dad. When Peter was in jail he would say he thought about how he treated me and he loved me.

I really thought he did care for me again, I really did. In a way, he did in his own twisted sick mind. When Peter had nothing he was a different person. We get on great, I was with the man I loved so much and Jordan had his Dad back in his life. Which all children do need. Life was great. It was a dream come true.

Every day I would try to be the best girlfriend in the world and not give him an excuse to hit me again. But bit by bit he became the old Peter again.

I could not believe I fell for all the things he said to me. He even told me he would love it us to get married. By God I was so happy. I tried and tried every day to treat him the way you would when you love someone. But it came natural to me. But started not to be good enough again. Once he had money in his pocket again, he started to beat me up. He made me feel like I was worthless again and I was not good enough to be Jordan's Alum.

Peter would say I could not talk normally or walk normally and I always made myself look like I was an idiot. I believed every word he said to me. I was an idiot and ugly and everything he said. Otherwise he would not say it. It was so easy to fall in the circle of hope again.

Every day it was getting worse. Peter's temper was so bad. I would only go to the shop and he would say I was meeting someone. I would not dare look at a man, which I would not anyway because I believe if you have a partner one is enough. I was and still am old fashioned. I believed when you had children with a man you don't go with another. I did not want to go with someone else. I would get beaten up for something he was doing and something I was not doing. I always thought he knew this but still he needed that power to feel good about himself. How can you hurt someone the way he hurt me every day all because you love being in control?

I will never understand this and never will. I tried so hard to understand and make excuses for him. I knew he did not have a good childhood, so I believed he became this monster because he was not loved as a child, But the thing was I did not have a good childhood either but I knew right from wrong like anyone does. But Peter thought he had the right to hurt me the way he did, because of his childhood or relationships before me. I tried so hard to understand because I wanted my son to have a Dad who was around.

For the past few years I had an eating disorder. This was due to the domestic violence affects your life in many ways.

Still today it affects my life. You never come out of the tunnel. You can see the light there but you can never get to the light, but knowing you are still trying to get there is a positive thing within yourself. If you stop believing in yourself and lose the faith and let the circle of hope loose, the light at the end of the tunnel gets further and further away. You try to stop it because it's getting further. But believing and having faith will bring you back to the light. If it had been done before, it could happen again, if you really wanted it to. But it's not as easy as it sounds.

Stef was a drug addict and she would come around to my house and ask for money and then while I would be going to the toilet, she would be filling up a carrier bag full of my stuff. I did not even realize this at the time, as my life was such a mess. I just wanted some company. But I had to pay the price each time. I thought she was being caring towards me. But no, she did not care really. I caught her with the bags one day, because she left her coat, so I opened my door to shout back at her. I would see her walking with one or two carriers. She would pretend not to hear me. This happened a few times. I realized she came with nothing. So where did she get the bags from? I used to sit there crying and when she knocked on the door I was grateful to see her. But it cost me to have a conversation with her. NV hen Peter used to come he would ask "Where's my tools?" for example. I would say they were where he left them. Then he knew that my sister had been in and then I would get beaten up for her. This happened so many times until I realized she nicking stuff from my house and I could not believe it. I so shocked. She would see mw with black eyes etc., but she did not come to see me, she just came to see how much she could get each time. My sister was a drug addict for eight years already. I knew I should not have trusted her, as children never got on. But I just expected more from her. She was always jealous of me and tried to ruin everything I had. All my life she would do this to me. As a kid she would lie and get away with it. As long as she got her own way she did not care who got in the way.

My sister worked as a prostitute. She would knock on Peter was there and she would come in with short skirts and knee high boots. I used to feel jealous in a because I would see Peter looking at her legs. The thing was she knew what she was doing and in front of me. But yet she did not care. She would keep bending down, knowing everyone was watching. She loved the attention, but I did not realize she was seeing Peter behind my back at this point. That's why she would do the things she did and get away with it.

Peter and his friends would be sitting most nights playing on the PSI. Playing football. When the time come for meal times I would cook for his friends too. Cooking for six people at a time became normal for me. His friends were grateful but to Peter it was normal for me being a slave and doing everything while he sat on his ass! His friends say "thank you". Peter would just look and smile or not say anything, because he is God you know! In his dreams anyway. Like I said, "idiot man"!

When I used to do everything, his friends would notice and when Peter was shouting at me his friend knew it was for no reason. Peter liked to feel good in that way. But his friends were my friends too in a way. but not all. They would look at him. Peter did not like it when his friends did this. It made him look bad. But so it should!

Well 27 April was my mum's birthday. I put a long-to-the-ankle woolen dress on. It was polo neck, but it fitted to me. Yes, it did look nice but I wanted to look nice, it was my Mum's birthday. We grew up to look nice on birthdays, anyone's birthday. We always made an effort to look nice. But to Peter I was going to meet someone.

So there I ready to go and get some flowers and he turned to say, "Where are you going like that?"

He laughed at me! He thought I was lying. But I really think he knew I would not go with anyone else. It was just to start. He was probably just miserable and he took it out on me.

He shouted at me, "You are not going anywhere!" I said, "1Vhy?"

"No, I'm not stupid, you slag!"

I hated him for this. A stone heart. I would have to sit there whilst Peter was shouting at me. I would always wait for him to get angrier because I knew he would start to hit me or kick me or to throw objects that hurt my head. I never did anything wrong and I am sitting there. Crying and scared, I would have to suffer for something I never did. But yet again it was him behind my back. All because he was doing something on me, I suffered a lot of heartache that was physical abuse. Why is that? He may be feeling guilty or he was very aware of everything. So if there was a chance he would be able to stop me from doing something positive or if I had to go out, he did. But if it was something for him he would let me. If there was a queue at the shop, I felt like I had a panic attack, because I Peter time me.

Thinking about it all at this time, I thought, "To waste your life and be scared and not knowing what's going to happen next is NOT RIGHT!" Please think and say to yourself 'I don't deserve this'. Please don't let go of your own life to save another's if they don't deserve this. Look yourself in the mirror and say "I'm a person and not a dog."

Well I tried to be as quick as I could at the shop. I hated it so much when there was a queue. I hated it so much I had to fit everything in this bubble of mine just to fight for my life every day.

Just to be able to relax in life would be great. I have to think about everything I do. I have to be careful the way I walk, the way I talk and dress, If I see anyone, I would not talk to them because I could not have a friend. It was OK for him to have friends but me, that's another story.

As time went by, I thought it's not fair what he was doing. But I had no friends to help me get away from him because all of them were scared of Peter. It would have to be a good plan to get away. I would have to pick the right time. My son will end up like his Dad if I don't do anything. Please God help me, I don't want my son to be like his father, please help me get away from him one day, please God. I beg you that you give me that strength for my son and to save him. There is no way I want my son to be a woman beater, NO NO NO NO.

I would beg myself to realize more and to be able to get away from him. It will happen one day I hope. I will do it for my son. Not myself, my son deserves more in life. and I hope to God I give him the life he deserves. Far away from his Dad. That is the way it must happen to save my son.

I would be ironing or doing the dishes and I think of different ways I could get from Peter. But I never had the courage to go through with it. But one day I will for my son. He is too beautiful to be a woman beater. He is my sexy little man!

Well it was time for Jordan to start nursery. I to cry. My God, it was now time for him to start out in the big wide world. His first time at nursery. He's left alone until I go and pick him up. Think about it, they are on their own. here they will have to stick up for themselves. So, yes it is the first time they go out in the big wide world. In my head it was so emotional for me, like the just blew up. I was that sad but happy at the same time. He is the only person who really loves me for real. I never want to lose him, and no way was I going to lose him to Peter. He wasn't going to destroy my son's life as well as mine.

CHAPTER 12

My son

My courage was getting stronger. My thoughts to Mum one day were still alive in my head. The seed I wanted to grow was starting. It starts forming your courage, which also starts your faith growing too. Even if I don't run away today, there are always other days I may get the courage. But I knew I would get to that point one day. But I never knew when. It is something you can't really plan. It goes with you when you are ready and when you realize it is not a life for yourself or your children. I wish I had thought about not having kids with Peter. I should have realized sooner and not bring an innocent soul to suffer.

He never stopped hitting me when I had my son. So why did I think having a child might stop him? I must have had my head in the clouds. But at least I realize now. That is what important today not yesterday but today. But realizing you want to get away is not the same as actually doing it. Until I have that courage I will have still suffered every day until that great morning or day. My son will suffer too. This made me feel like I was being cruel to my son. I think this is why my courage and faith started to grow enough to run for our lives. hat a miracle. Thank you God xx.

When I realized I did really want to do it, I felt so Scared for even thinking it. But I was very proud of myself for even thinking it. You go girl! Hooray! Ahh ahh!

But until that thankful morning, life had to carry on

Jordan started to go to nursery just in the morning twice a week. Then soon after every day. My beautiful gorgeous son was growing up and I was really worried I would lose him. He had true love for me as well as me for him. Every day I would wonder what our lives would be like without Peter in it. I needed to keep the faith I had. That will save our lives one day. I wished and never gave up.

At this point Peter would tell him not to listen to me. Jordan did not know to think, but his Dad tried to think for him and tell him not to listen to me and tell him I wasn't good enough to be his mum. This idiot man called his Dad tried to tell him I was not his Mum. This made me angry. How dare he do that. My hate grew stronger for him and my courage and faith was growing more and more. I will NOT let him take my son away from me again, EVER AGAIN. I won't let him. This I knew. But how was a big question.

Well, Jordan was getting older. I took thousands of pictures of him. I did not miss a minute of his life. My son gave me my faith and I returned the love by saving him from his Dad. Once I'm gone I will try my best.

Peter and his friends still came around and I try my best not to talk to them because of Peter and his green-eyed monster. But Peter started to bring girls back to my house and Peter would always spend time on his own with them. I did not realize he bringing his girlfriend's home. The girls knew who I was. But they pretended to be a friend and they had a boyfriend. But I used to wonder why they tell me this. I go bed not too late because of getting up in the morning for Jordan. I would wake up in the morning Peter next to me but the girl the settee. How would 1 not realize? It really makes me feel stupid because I should have realized. But you mustn't blame yourself at all. It is them being heartless and they DON'T deserve your love. You don't realize because it's downright nasty, sick and disgusting. How dare he do this to me.

The girls on the settee would go as soon as they up. But sometimes I was there making them a cup of tea in the morning. Without realizing that Peter spent the night with them, and in my own home! It's sick, how could he do such a thing?

If I got up in the morning and they were asleep on the settee, she would say sorry. Then I never realized Peter did not always come to bed and he said he'd been awake all night. He would say if a girl was on the settee when I woke up that she had fallen out with her boyfriend and got locked out. Me, being an idiot and believing what he was telling me, would say "That's OK, do you want a cuppa?"

I feel sick still to this day that Peter did this to me. I loved him so much even if he beat me all the time. But YES love makes you blind. But I do realize what a cruel act this was, even for Peter. WHY does he keep hurting me like this? I was the only person who really loved him. Everybody else used him for his money.

Peter could be very cruel. He would say I'm too thick to be Jordan's Mum and he will make me feel ashamed for being his Mum. He also said that when Jordan gets older and he's growing up he will be embarrassed of me. He said a lot of things to me. The only thing in my life which I care about is my son. I wanted him to love me and care for me. I did not want him to be like his Dad. So I took some tablets to kill myself. I had had enough. My life was so shit and if the only person loved me will feel ashamed of me then I wanted to be dead.

Whilst taking the tablets I was crying for my son. I would take them and cry. Thinking that Jordan will be ashamed of me was so hurtful. He deserves the best I can do for him, but if I'm not looking after him properly and not being a proper Mum, I decided the best thing to do was for me to die, if it's the best thing for my son I will do it and take as many tablets as I could — 78 tablets altogether. I fell asleep. But I woke up.

This was very WRONG of me. If I loved my son the way I said I did, then what about when he wakes up in the morning and he wants me and I am dead? How upsetting that would be for my child. I realized my mistake and I got to save my son in the end I was taking the tablets for nothing. Please DON'T ever do this for your child or children. Think about them if you love them.

CHAPTER 13

Mother's Day

It was Mother's Day and I got ready to go to my Stepdad's with Jordan, to go to the crematorium to give my Mum some flowers. Peter asked me where I thought I was going.

Putting my lipstick on I said, "I'm going to give some flowers to my Slum with my Stepdad and Jordan.

Yeah right! You are not going anywhere," Peter said.

Yet again he stopped me from going to see my Stepdad and I had to obey him like a dog. I just sat there and prayed to my Mum, saying that I love you lots Mother dude and happy Mother's Day xx.

Peter made me feel like I was dead inside. Fighting for my life every day was making me feel weak. Like I had nothing to live for. I had to ask permission for everything. Like he was a God. I started to hate him more. I started to gain my courage and my faith getting stronger. I knew from that point I wouldn't take this forever and one day I will be gone with Jordan.

When, where and what I was going to do, I did not know. Stopping me from seeing my Mum I knew could not take it and wouldn't take it, Peter was accusing me all day that I was going to meet someone, man he said.

He would start shouting "Who is he? Tell me who he is NOW!"

I kept saying, "I am not going to meet anyone except my Stepdad to go to the crem"

"How stupid do you think I am?" he shouted

"Honest, just my Stepdad," I beg him, "that is all I am going to do."

"No, no, no. Don't lie to me ill front of my face!"

He would quickly head butt me in my face. All I could see was flashes, white flashes. I did not feel the pain straight away with my fear. I would look in the mirror. Yet again another tooth loose and a black eye. I did nothing wrong. He did all this for no reason. I did not dare to fart in front of him.

Never mind having a quickie with another man.

By now I would be sitting there crying and wouldn't dare say a word until he stopped going on. If he saw that I was scared most of the time, he would say, why are you scared? Done something wrong?" I said I was not going to meet anyone, I thought in my head. I knew he would beat me up for something I did not do. I did not dare to breathe wrong. I would be sitting there like a scared rat.

Only talking when I was allowed to. I could feel the fear in me, every bone felt like it was shaking. On and on and on all day long. All for nothing. I've done nothing and still get treated like this! WHY? This is not fair. Peter would like to sit in the bedroom an d watch TV. He said because he felt more comfortable. It started just a day or two during the week and then it got to every day. J hated it.

Peter went to sit upstairs. Yes, I had to go too. He made me feel like a little child, or a dog who had to obey. If one of his friends was there I had no choice but to go with him, More and more each day I started to hate Peter. I could not do what I wanted in my own home. All because he let his friends in. But his friend would be here every day. He's had nowhere to go. Peter used to call him his "joey" slave in other words. Asked him to do a lot of things. But if he let one of his friends in the house, he should trust them enough not to go with me (like I would anyway). NOT! Peter ruled every step of my life, every breath, even every fart. It felt like it anyway! I joke about this but it was not funny at the time.

CHAPTER 14

Is this really my life now?

It was time to get Jordan from school. Peter would not let me go to pick him up. He would not let me out of the bedroom. I had to ask for permission to go to the toilet. Peter told me I was not allowed to take

Jordan to school or pick him up any more. I was not to have anything to do with Jordan from now.

"You are useless. Jordan will learn you are not his Mum. I will find a proper woman to be my son's Mum. Not you."

He would shut the door and shout, "Stay in here, don't try to run off or anything."

"OK."

Bang the door went. I would have to sit there and listen to Jordan in the house and I was not allowed to talk to him or play with him or see him full stop. I would be dying inside. My heart ached so much. I had to wait for Peter to come back upstairs. He came in and I said I can't cope with not having anything to do with Jordan. It was hurting me so much.

"You can't make me stay in this room."

Peter said, "Oh yeah who are you missing then?

I said "Only Jordan, Peter. This is not right. How can you do this to me?"

I went to walk out of the bedroom and he laid on the side of the bed which was closest to the door. As I was just going to reach for the door handle he grabbed my arm and pulled me down and kneed the left side of my head.

My head was covered in blood. My God blood out like it was a fountain. I started to scream. My face covered in blood. I was so scared. Thought I was going to die. I started to open the door and ran screaming to the bathroom. Peter's friend downstairs was shouting at the bottom of the stairs asking if I was OK. Peter, I think, just sat there. He did not try to help me. All of this and all I wanted to do was go and see my Mum. I kept being hurt for something I did not do. I prayed to God asking him to help me.

I walked around with this bandage wrapped around my head for the rest of that day. Thank God some of his friends knocked on the door, so he had to go downstairs and so could I. But only after Jordan went to bed. Peter did look like he was going mad. His friends knew what went on because Laz his friend who normally stayed here, would have told them. They looked at Peter wondering why he was being so cruel. He blamed me for everything that went wrong. Also I was seeing people behind his back, he thought. I think because he was cruel and his friends would look at him like it too. He did not like it, and he took it out on me. Jordan was young so I could even pretend and say I was just playing with the bandage on my head. But

Peter would not let me see him anyway. I knew this could not carry on like this.

I would make out I was cleaning in the kitchen and I would be crying and crying. I could not see my son or see my Stepdad. I just stopped going to see him because of Peter. I could not tell him why. Thinking he would have been upset because I let him down that day, upset me even more. What was I supposed to do? Now if I was super woman I would not have this problem!

What a shame! I could not hurt another person like this but Peter was not a person, he was a thing!

When his friends were here I would say I was going to the toilet, but I would sneak to see Jordan. Once he was just sitting there playing and I asked him if we could color in a picture together. I cherished every second and I would be crying inside. Peter came to realize this so he would time me and wait at the living room door for me. I could not sneak and see my son any more. Peter was so cruel. How could you do this?

But Peter could not carry this on. Too many people were knowing Peter was stopping me. I think that's why Peter started to let me see my son again. I was not bothered why. I was next to my son playing whenever I liked. It was super cool. I thanked God for this. I started to take Sambo the dog for a walk so I would pick up Jordan from school and we would go up the Parkall fields. It was amazing, we would run to the top of the bank and roll down. We all had great fun. It was nice. Then we would stand in a line (me, Jordan and Sambo) and start running down the hill. When you are running downhill and you can't stop laughing, you can trip and roll down. At the end of the race down the hill. Sambo always came first. But it was so much fun. Sambo loved it and so did me and Jordan. It was something to look forward to.

I would start to get ready to pick up Jordan from school and Sambo knew because he was getting used to it and as he got used to it, you would hear him getting excited knowing he's going out soon.

But no, Peter had to put a stop to that too. It broke my heart. It was so nice and enjoyable for us and he had to stop all the fun. Peter always did. Samb0 would start whining when it was time to get Jordan. I hated Peter, he spoiled everything good for me.

Peter beat me up because he said I was meeting someone up the fields. I said we were just having He would say "Who were you having fun with? fun. Admit who you were meeting!" I would beg to Peter that I was only with Jordan and Sambo. He would start shouting, "Tell me the truth!"

Yet again I would be sitting there crying, begging him I was telling the truth. But he stopped me again seeing Jordan and I would have to stop in the bedroom again.

One day I could not take it anymore and I was crying so much, listening to Jordan. So one day I wanted to try to kill myself again. I had no escape. Locked up like an animal. I went to the bathroom crying and I shut the bathroom door, wondering what I was going to do. I could not climb out of the window. I saw the bleach under the sink and I started to drink it. I did not drink much. I was crying so much. I thought if I showed Peter I would rather die than live with him he might ease off a bit. I walked back in the bedroom telling him I had had enough so I drank some bleach. He shouted "What?"

I started to tell him that I had done nothing on him with his friends and he was making me suffer for something I did not do. You are evil.

"Shut up!" he would say.

He kicked me and punched me a couple of times to make sure I did shut up.

One-day Peter had to let me go and pick up Jordan, as One of the teachers wanted to talk to me. So I was able to take Jordan school and pick him up for a little while after this. I was happy with that. When I got back I would have to go straight back upstairs to the bedroom to Peter, if Laz was there. I would be just sitting there looking at the walls until Peter woke up. I could not do anything. I started to hate him so much for being so cruel to me. All because of the friend's h let in the house I had to suffer. Everything was being cruel to me. What was I supposed to do?

My hate for Peter grew very strong. I could not let my son see me screaming and crying like this all the time. He will do the same. I wanted to stop the circle My son is never going to be a woman beater like his Dad and Granddad and so forth. NO WAY my son will become that cruel. I had to get strong to leave Peter and this time leave for good. How was I going to do it? I would have ideas. But it became so hard. I had to think of something. My son will suffer and no way that was going to happen.

I can remember one day, Peter was asleep and I broke a bottle of sterilized milk. I took the top part of the bottle which was very sharp and I put it in my pocket. I cleaned up the rest of the glass and went up to Peter. I was lying next to him with this glass inches away from his neck. I so wanted to hurt him the way he was hurting me and my son. But if I stuck that in Peter's neck I would have been in prison now. How was I supposed to help Jordan if I was locked up? so I took the broken part of the bottle wrapped it up and put it in the rubbish. I really scared myself. For something I so wanted to do, because I can't take it anymore, I just couldn't.

I realized what measures I nearly took because Peter was so cruel. I did actually scare myself. Thinking about it, if Peter had opened his eyes and seen what I wanted to do he could have taken the glass from me and done it to me. I was so lucky that day. God really helped when I needed it. I thank God because I was not a murderer. But nearly acted like one. All because of Peter. I was not going to be locked up and my life taken away from me and ruined because Peter is a woman beater. It would wreck Jordan's life. I had to think about my son before myself. As a parent, it's your job as a mother. Well, I think it's my job. I was not about to spoil my chance of saving my son's life. Karma has a lot to say for itself. Please believe and see it for yourself. It's a great thing to have faith which helps with your courage also, really it does! It did me anyway.

CHAPTER 15

Peter's games

My sister still came around, sometimes she sat with Peter in our bedroom. But so did some other girls. I would be sitting with Jordan. Peter started to sit upstairs a lot. So some of the times his friends would too. Great, I thought, I can't get told I'm trying to get off with anyone now. There was only one toilet so I had to go upstairs to go there. That's all. Peter used to shut the door so I just went to the toilet and back down. Yes, it hurt but I was just happy not being shouted at or beaten up. Sometimes at night they came down, but like I said I did not go to bed too late because I had to get up for Jordan.

But one-day Peter told me, "Get in the car." I never did anything wrong but felt scared as soon has he said it.

I said, "What about Jordan?"

"Laz has got him."

So there I went and did what I was told. I opened the car door shaking. I was wondering what was going on and what was wrong with Peter. I'd been doing the ironing all day, I prayed that he wouldn't hurt me. I sat in the car and smiled to see what reaction I was going to get.

"Put your seat belt on and hold on," he said.

"Hold on, oh God now what?" I thought.

He started the car and by now he could see I was worried. But he knew I was waiting to see what I'd

But even though I hadn't done anything wrong, still scared for my life.

"What you scared for?" he said. "I thought you 'd done nothing wrong?"

said you

"Yes, that is true. I have not. Please believe me."

He was going slow, but as soon as I said that he turned his head like Chuckie and just looked at me so evilly. He put his foot down. He was going about 120mph up a 30mph road. My life went past me and the houses on each side were too.

We came to the end of the road and I just put my hands over my eyes. He slowed down enough to stop there. It was all just to scare me to death. Another sick joke of his to get me to feel scared for something I did not do.

We got out of the car. I was shaking and crying.

Peter laughed, saying "Did you enjoy that?"

It was all a big game to him, I think to make himself feel better. He is a strange person all right.

He turned around to me and got serious and shouted, "Tell me now who are you seeing?"

I just said, "You just scared me to death for something I did not do wrong. This is not fair."

He said, "Shut up and get in the house."

I turned around and walked slowly into the house crying because I knew what was going to happen, and I did not do anything wrong. Please help me God.

I put my foot in the front door of the house and Peter shut his car door so hard it made me jump. I did not know what to think. I did nothing wrong but was sitting here scared to death. It's just how long he teases me before he beats me. But you could all know because he would get angrier. Then I knew It would not be long now. I was so scared, my heart was shaking, my whole body would start to shake then my breath would start going faster and faster. But at the same time I could not show this to peter too much because he would say it's a sign I'm guilty for something. I had to control my breathing whilst trying to save my life, begging him I did not do anything wrong.

"LIAR," he shouted.

Then I cried more and he started taking the micky out of me because I was crying.

He started to tell me what a fool I was and nobody really likes me. They are just pretending. But whilst he would be shouting at me sometimes I would just stare at his mouth. As time went by I was thinking and realizing that what he was saying to me, it was the opposite.

People started to realize I never two-timed Peter at all. But he would still beat me for it. But the friends he was saying about were his friends that stopped coming around. That's why he would shout.

He would start shouting at me that I'm going around their house when I take the dog for a walk or when I go to the shop. I would beg to him that I was not doing anything wrong. At that point I'd been with Peter for five years.

For the rest of the day I could not have anything to do with Jordan at all because he said I'm a tart. So I had to stay in the bedroom again. All night. I would hear Jordan going to bed and I would cry. I was sick of all the pain and I was sick of crying. I'd done nothing wrong. I would sit on the bed just looking at the wall. Wondering when Peter was going to come up and beat me for something I did not do.

I would pray to God and my Mum and Dad. I would tell them I'm so sorry, I did not want to be failure. I would cry and tell them sorry because I would tell them, one day it might be different, I don't know when. Or even if.

I started to think about the day I had and Peter driving like a mad man. We could have got killed, all because he two-timed me for years and now he accused me of things he's done. But I could not sit there for the rest of my life and not be able to be without my son. He truly loved me and that's a special love and I was not going to waste it. I knew still at that point I would get away from Peter and I would wonder how life would be without him and me and Jordan playing all the time and being happy. I always wondered what it would feel like.

When Peter started to walk up the stairs my heart would be going 100mph. He walked in the bedroom with a smile.

"You all right?"

I said, "Yes thanks."

He started to say, "I know you have been wondering when I was coming upstairs and what I was going to be like with you, but I wanted to say sorry for today. I know now, so please don't worry."

I think I just stared at him and my heart stopped. I could not believe my ears.

I said, "Pinch me but not hard."

He laughed. "Why?"

"I'm just so happy that you said what you did, and not blaming me for something I didn't do. It's great. Hooray!„

Peter just laughed. I think I died and went to heaven. This was not normal. But we stopped going on about it all and watched a video and enjoyed the night. He said such lovely things to me that night. did say sorry a few times too. It was great!

Peter fell asleep and I went downstairs, to start bacon and egg sandwich for Peter and myself. Before I left the room I did try to wake him, but he was not waking up. I kept saying "Do you want a sandwich?" But I had no answer, so I just carried on with it. 1 was hungry and I wanted to make an effort for him, even though it was 2am. I was happy and I tried to show it back. I went to the bottom of the stairs and shouted up "Peter are you awake?" No answer so I just went back in the kitchen. His friend Laz was asleep on the settee.

I don't think he was asleep, but Peter would forget that when he shouted at me people can hear him. I think he forgot that. I had to walk through the living room to get to the kitchen. I could smell smoke so knew he had turned everything off and pretended to be asleep because he knew Peter would shout at me. I did think that was kind. But I stayed in the kitchen and did not dare go in the living room. I shut the door and cleaned the cooker. I cooked the bacon and went upstairs a few times but Peter still was asleep. So I just carried on in the kitchen and made sure the door was shut. I heard Peter was up so I rushed his sandwich because I started to panic. I don't know why after having a good night with him. I just knew what he was thinking.

So, I rushed his sandwich and forgot to put on brown sauce and did not cut his sandwich. I could not believe it. Fancy forgetting that. It was because I was panicking. So I gave him his sandwich but started to cook a bit more so I rushed to give him his sandwich and ran back downstairs.

He shouted to me, "What have you been up to?"

"Oh, no," I thought.

I knew I had done nothing wrong and so did his but he was shouting and Laz downstairs could hear

"I was trying to wake you!"

I said. "Liar.'" he shouted.

"I was only cleaning the cooker after I cooked the bacon because you were asleep. Otherwise I wouldn't have been cleaning up at this hour. I'm happy we had a good night and wanted to make an effort instead of having cereal."

"Liar!"

I started to stutter.

"It's because you are guilty," he said.

"I'm just upset because of what you are saying and I have done nothing wrong."

"Liar!

He got up and went downstairs. Laz was pretending to be asleep for me so I did not get in trouble, but I did anyway. When Peter went down he still pretended to be asleep and Peter said he was pretending because he was guilty. I thought no way, not again. I just wanted to be dead, but I wanted to see my son so I can't be dead now, can I? I was sick of everything, I've done nothing wrong. I can't just walk around my house and do what I want. I started to hate him more and more and more.

Was it just me, was I never meant to be happy or what?

When he came upstairs he just laughed and said, "Is he for real? He is just pretending, do you both think I'm that stupid?"

I kept on and on and on saying I had done nothing Wrong.

He was shouting, "How could you do this to me in our home. Are you that heartless? You dirty person!"

He started to hit me and kick me and punch me for nothing. I had done nothing wrong again. "I'm leaving. had enough," I said.

"You can go," he said. "But you are not taking Jordan."

I just wanted to go because I was getting beaten up for nothing.

He said, "l know you are guilty now and you can't live yourself can you?"

I said, "No, that is not it at all."

"You can keep joking yourself but you can't fool me. Just remember that."

Some of his friends started to knock on the door.

He was shouting "You dirty person. You went with Laz behind my back."

He shouted this to everyone and he pulled my jeans down so he could put his hand down my knickers, and put his hand in. When he pulled his hand away from my knickers in front of everyone and smelled his hand he said that was not the smell of me.

"You dirty person!"

In front of everyone I pulled my jeans up and ran out of the door and cried my eyes out, walking up to my Stepdad's.

I walked up the road wondering what was going to happen now, what about Jordan. I had run off without him. What am I going to do now? I could not believe what I just went through. But the thing is, it's all for nothing. I'm repeatedly getting beaten up for something I've not done. What is he trying to prove? Why does he have to act like he's God? He's a heartless piece of nothing. That's what he is, NOTHING!

CHAPTER 16

Peter's stone heart

He's got to try to prove that his mistakes are all my fault. He has to blame someone else because he HIM that is guilty. I dare not breathe wrong in front of him and he's telling me I went with another man in the same house. Oh yeah, as if I would dare. I'm too scared to fart. Never mind going with another man. I think it's a joke or something. It doesn't make sense to me. Why go to this length to prove I'm the dirty person? But he KNOWS and KNEW it was HIM. He is a heartless piece of nothing like I said. How can I carry on this life? I can't. And WON'T. I will fight for my son. He gave me my courage and faith and I have the power to run for my life — well our lives - and NEVER go back.

I walked up the road looking like a tramp. I hadn't had any sleep all night and I looked like my twin sister a druggie — and I hated that because we were twins. I looked thin because I was not eating properly, not because I was a druggie. But the estate I was brought up in was rough. The people who took drugs knew I was not a druggie. But to normal people, like my neighbors or strangers, I would look like a druggie. Everyone is stereotyped, and no one can deny the truth. First looks of someone and you look like a tramp or a druggie. You get looked down at. But in truth I never took the drugs. But they did not know this as they did not know me. But the world is a cruel place. You can't judge a book by the cover.

I look at people when they dye their hair pink bright red and think, "Good for them." You can't keep going through life worrying what the next person thinks of you. If they don't like you, say then it's their loss and get on with your life. You can't waste your life not being able to do what you want to. You might as well be caged in a big cage and give up your life. But I can't give up and won't for my son. He's too important to me. I was blessed with such a wise and beautiful •son. But everyone makes mistakes and lies to themselves about how things went in their lives. But one thing was always proven and that was the love I had for my son. I WILL save him from his Dad. I WILL.

I carried on to my Stepdad's, knowing I will have to go back for Jordan. I knew that from the time I stepped out of that house without him. To me now Peter was the Devil. and he's NOT getting my son.

I looked a mess and heartbroken. I could not stop crying. I was worried my Stepdad also thought I was on drugs like my twin sister because I looked just like her. I tried to feel what it was like looking at me like that, and yes I looked a druggie. Just like Peter tried to portray me. Just so he looked the poor thing and he got attention. I hate you Peter!

More than hate it was now. I could not believe how I felt. All because of Peter. He is the one who was guilty and I'm sick of people thinking the wrong thing about me. People did see Peter with other girls. So Peter could not deny that. He tried so hard to look like it was me, that it was all my own fault. But the thing was it was all HIS!

The harder Peter tried to prove I was the baddie, the more people did not believe him. But now the people from the streets of Bentilee knew it was NOT me. Everyone knew what he did to me. How can he prove that he's the good one? People realized that it was not your fault and it's great when people know the truth. Hooray, people know it was not me! At last!!

I do love karma, thank you x

I stayed with my Stepdad for about three nights. But I was going around the school where Jordan was just to watch him every day. I would get there before 12pm and wait for him to come out on to the playground after school dinner. I did this every day while I was away from him. I would just sit in the park next to the school after just crying. Not knowing what was going to happen.

On the fourth day, myself and my Stepdad were on the way to the big shops when we saw Peter. He went past us then turned around in the car. I knew he would stop at the bus stop we were waiting at.

I just looked at my Stepdad. I was sorry for my Stepdad, but I had to go back for my son. I didn't think it was fair that I only went to my Stepdad's when I fell out with Peter. But I could not go when I wanted because of Peter. He tried to make my Stepdad think I did not care for him and tried to make me look so bad that he did not want anything to do with me. That was Peter's plan all along. But Peter was clever at lying and people always fell for it. Even my Stepdad in the end thought I was a bad one. Peter would tell them I was on drugs and I came to realize that Peter had an addiction to drugs himself and I could not believe it. I did not realize this until I left. Right at the beginning at the flat it was Peter with the beer and he became an alcoholic. I paid for loving him. Time and time again. When would time just stop for me? Just to let me go free with my son?

Peter gave me a lift to the big shops whilst my Stepdad waited for the bus. So I waited at the bus stop at the big shops for my Stepdad to get there and to get off the bus with Peter.

I knew my Stepdad would not be happy but I didn't realize that Peter had been up to his flat and told my Stepdad to tell me to come back or he would break all his windows.

But I did not know this till after my Stepdad stopped talking to me. Peter told me. He would have made my Stepdad so scared and I did not know and it was all my fault. I did not mean to cause him any harm. He did realize this and knew it was Peter and not me at that point anyway. Whilst waiting for the bus to stop, Peter was telling me about Jordan and how he was missing me. God, I wanted go right there and then to see him. Go to see my beautiful son. Peter knew what he was saying. He said he tried to get Jordan a new mum but Jordan wanted me, his real mum.

I cried at that point. Being loved was so lovely by my son. Love comes in many ways.

I knew my son loved me and being told he wanted me felt so beautiful. Being loved for real is fantastic, gorgeous, beautiful and heart-warming. I walked around the shops with my Stepdad in a world of my own. I tried to tell him what he said, but he knew I would go back when Jordan was involved. I tried saying I had to go back for my son. He just said it was OK. I thanked him. I never thought that he was probably wondering how long he would get to see me and Jordan again. It must have been upsetting for him. This is what happens when you are in the circle of hope. It is not just you that gets hurt. Your family hurts too. But only because they love and care for you and they don't want to see you hurt.

From another point of view. Try thinking it's your child getting hurt every day. Would you want this for your child? How would you feel when you are the parent? So, without realizing it, everybody fits in that circle of hope. Plus, your parents and anyone that cares for you will hope too. How would you get your child to stop getting hurt without getting pushed away, because when they say this to you don't realize it's because they care and if they did not, they would say anything at all? So please think about this and please don't lose your family over a bully. You WILL come to realize they were right and even though you were hoping they weren't, they are. PLEASE LISTEN TO THEM, PLEASE.

Think about what everyone says, don't just disregard it because you don't agree with it. Remember everything and think about it please, because everyone can't be wrong except you. But this is why they say "love makes you blind". Sometimes it's hard to learn from your mistakes. But please learn "leopards don't change their spots". It's very rare they do and if they do, well you are one of the lucky ones. But nine times out often they don't. Yes, really! Don't let your heart give in that easy, please, like I did.

Anyway, as I was saying. I was telling my Stepdad that I had arranged for Peter to come and pick me up later that day and that I was really missing Jordan.

He said, "If you think it's the right thing to do, that's up to you."

"OK."

I did not realize that was going be the last time I would see him to talk to. Peter stopped me from doing everything. He moved from his flat because of Peter and the trouble I caused him. I was happy he was with his daughters and knew they would look after him. The way your parents deserve when getting older. I could not do that for him. I will always love my Stepdad and miss him. I think he is 72 years old now. I don't think I will ever see him again. Please don't let this happen to you.

Later that day Peter came to pick me up and I hugged my Stepdad and ran to the car. I could not wait to see Jordan. Peter was nice for a few days but everything went back to normal. Peter kept asking me why I ran off like that.

I said, "Peter, you put your hands down my knickers to prove a point to yourself and your friends, but I never did anything to you to prove."

He asked me, "Did you practice that?"

Nothing I said was going to change his mind.

I ended up saying, "You will only know the truth when you die, if you won't believe me now." I got a big slap across my face.

"You tart! Now I know you went with Laz."

"You won't believe a word I say to you."

That was the last thing I could think of to say. SLAP SLAP!

"Do you think I'm that stupid?" 'I'm stupid for loving you."

HIT and A KICK.

I saw stars again in my eyes and my body hurt all over. He went downstairs and I could not live like this any more so I jumped out of the window. But Peter heard me and ran out of the front door. Seconds behind me he was. He caught up with me and I was back to the house like 1 was a little girlie. A names 1 was calling him.

I started to save again my "runaway money"- and I had a post office account, and I had to hide the book anywhere I could and keep swapping places so peter did not find it. But when I ran off I was trying to stick the book in my bra or somewhere so Peter could not see it. I nearly got caught with it but didn't. Thank you, God. I hid that book everywhere around my house. I needed to make sure I had money for myself and Jordan before I left and this time I hoped it was for good.

I ran off with Jordan and went to Southampton where my older sister lived. I stayed with her for two or three days and then got a place in a shared house. it was a refuge for women suffering from domestic violence. I did not like it there as I was a quiet person and some people can think that's because you are weak and can take advantage. I started to feel uncomfortable in the house. Jordan was the youngest there. It was soon to be Christmas so I decided to leave and went back to Peter. Back to my house. It was only after two weeks when I decided to go back.

I needed to make sure I did it right next time and NOT come back. Jordan was happy to be back because of all his toys. I started to think how was I going do it right and not come back. It seemed harder and harder the more I thought about it.

I got Jordan back in the nursery and carried on with my beautiful life (I wished!). Peter's friends came around as normal and the hate for Peter just grew and grew and grew.

Jordan was getting older, My God, he is so beautiful. He will break some hearts when he gets older. He's got his looks from me you know! Haha! He's becoming a young man now. He will be starting primary school and he will be four years old. Wow! I can't believe how time can fly. This year was like no other. The same getting beaten up for nothing. God if I blinked wrong I had a slap or kick. Peter also kept telling Jordan not to do what I say and that I'm not his real Mum. This must have been confusing to Jordan and it was not fair of Peter to say it to him. He's nearly four years old and his Dad keeps saying things like this to him.

Jordan was getting really naughty when he was with me. But an angel for his Dad. But he was only naughty for me because of Peter his idiot of a Dad who kept saying things to him. Jordan was very spoilt and I said I always wanted my child to be spoilt because I was not as a child. But naughtiness comes from being spoilt. Thinking they must get their way each time. Peter did that on purpose but I had to suffer all the naughtiness because of Peter. God, I hated him so much. How dare he keep trying to get Jordan to hate me. Putting ideas in his head. I can't wait to leave this house, I just can't.

I became to think Peter was saying things on purpose so I would keep running off. I later got told how each time I ran off my twin sister Stef used to go around. They were seeing each other for a while before I even left Stoke for good. But the thing was that Peter was seeing other girls too. Was my sister to think she was the only one? She's a fool if she did. When I got told this I could not believe my ears. My sister would do this to me? How cruel. She's got a black heart.

Soon it will be Christmas. Peter went bust and he kept taking my money off me and leaving me with 120 for shopping for a week. He would say, "Don't worry, I will get some more money." Really, I did not have a choice. But the thing was my son was not going to go without because his Dad was so selfish. Yes, Jordan was only young but he deserved his treats like crisps and ice cream etc. I knew I was going to leave soon but did not know when. I sent my post office book to my older sister Tracy so she could save it for me. There was money in the account and CIOO in the book which I did not have time to go to the post office to put it in because Peter would time me going to the shop and there was a big queue.

I knew it was time for me and Jordan to leave this house. I won't have my son going without for anyone. So when Peter was moaning he had no money I suggested selling this and that around the house because I knew I would not be able to take it with me. He thought he was so clever, but for a change it was me. In your face! Because I'm going to hit the road Jack!

We needed to get money from somewhere because we would run out of milk and food. That is how bad Peter got. He was so selfish. If I was to stay I would have hardly anything left after Peter sold it all. Jordan had a jeep. Massive, it was. Like a real little jeep, it was. Peter sold it. I could not believe it. It was good in a way because I would not let him do this to my son and knew I would be gone sooner rather than later. He could hurt me, but never my son. Not like this. God, I called Peter some names! In my head, of course. It was funny when you think about it. Everything in life to Peter is a game and because my heart hurt too much and the hate was taking over and the protection of my son, I started to play the game knowing I did not love him anymore. It made me not scared of what he thought, because how dare he do this to my son. And he thinks he's going to get away with this? Yeah right, my time will come you idiot of a man and karma is great! She's great. In your face! Haha'.

I'd taken nearly eight years of Peter hitting me, but when the moment comes when he hurts my son in any way I was gone. But the more I started to hate Peter, the more I realized things. My God, what kind of fool have I been? As long as you realize, that is what matters. I knew it will be hard on my own but I was going to save my son from his Dad. You can bet on that.

I started to look at Peter in a different way. Did I need glasses?

Yeah, love is blind all right! But when I was realizing things, I felt so stupid and hurt. How could Peter have done what he's done to me? I hadn't deserved any of it. What makes a person's heart go bad and black inside? How could he? How could my sister do it to me too? How and what makes people turn evil?

CHAPTER 17

My Christmas

It was Christmas eve and Peter bought nothing for Jordan. I cashed my money and only had L20 to spend on Jordan. I was so heartbroken. I had to go the pound shop and I brought as many toys as I could. 1 wrapped them all up ashamed. Ashamed that life had got this low. Like I said, my son will not keep suffering because of his selfish Dad.

It was nearly tea time on Christmas Eve when my sister Stef knocked on the door. I was upstairs with peter at the time. Watching a bit of TV and just talking. It was nice for a change. But then he started an argument on purpose. But I did not know why. But he started an argument just so I would go downstairs. Then my sister went up and Peter said I could only come upstairs to go to the toilet. But if I knocked on the bedroom door he would beat me. So I sat there thinking was this right? Jordan would ask why his Auntie Stef was in bed with Daddy. I just said, "I don't know sweetheart, let's just watch TV my darling and turn it up."

So there was me and Jordan watching TV while they were in the bedroom together. I wanted the TV to be turned up because I did not want to hear any noise from that room. It made me feel sick. I did not know what's going on. But why should they hurt me so much like this? Why would they want to do this to me and not even care and come downstairs to get something then go back upstairs as if it was alright to treat me like I was invisible.

Sick people I feel they are. Always very selfish people Peter and Stef. Both have got black hearts.

As I was sitting there on the settee watching Tv with Jordan I was thinking how wrong this was and how was I supposed to act normally knowing what was really going on. I expected more of my sisters. But as I was sitting there, I thought it was a joke or something. Please can I wake up now! PLEASE!

Were they sitting in bed laughing at me? Thinking of the moment just hurt me more and pretending and playing games in my head is the way I survived it. Every time I needed to go to the toilet, each step up the stairs, just broke me more. Knowing what they were doing. I would look at the door when walking back down the stairs. Wondering what they were doing. But probably best if I did not know. As all of this is just sick. How could they? I don't think I could cry properly. I just could not believe it. How their black hearts got together to hurt me more.

In life I think, love, honesty and money makes the world go round. Good people, bad people it doesn't matter where you live. But family I think is precious. Yes, blood is thicker than water, but in my case the blood was not there, it had dried up. But the water just kept pouring. No blood, no heart, just themselves in their empty shells. The pain they cause other people is just normal to them. No one gets in their way. They've got black hearts and they don't even care. But people who have good hearts they try to destroy. The good are only weak to them. They pretend to have a good heart to get to know everything about you and to fool you, just to use against you. When you are getting weaker they are getting stronger. They love the power to crush your heart, just when they feel like it, it's just a game and a big fat joke on us. By loving them and trying more, you are obeying their call. It's very thrilling for them. Pay back to you for their own misery and mistakes. But I don't understand and never will. Why they look at the pain they are causing and carry on and on and on. WHY? When looking at Peter it was like he was empty, his heart had long gone. His eyes with such an empty stare.

Not able to show any emotion because their black hearts won't let them. But even a black heart could turn good. But misery and power is what they know to survive in life. They can control that. They think of the way to go and they are sticking with it. No matter what they do or say.

It was time for Jordan to go to bed. Jordan kept asking why Auntie Stef was in bed with Dad? I told him to ask his Dad. I didn't know why. I started playing with him. to change the subject.

After Jordan went to bed I lay on the settee in the living room in the dark, but left the kitchen light on so I did have a little light. I tried to get to sleep. Peter would not let me have any fags. I had to sit there with nothing, but with only my heart which can't stop beating with the pain.

My sister kept coming down the stairs, she gave me a couple of fags. Said she nicked them for me. But she had a Miss Shit attitude.

It was my house, my home and she was acting like the Queen Witch she is and was acting and saying are you OK. Only to tell Peter when she went back upstairs. So I just kept saying I was tired and wanted to go to sleep. She would say "Whatever". Each time one of them came downstairs, mainly my sister, my heart I think kept stopping with the pain. My sister with no remorse. She was so hurting me and even talking down to She stared me in the face talking to me, only to me. back up to Peter and she wondered why I did go really talk. Mmmmm let me think about that! Well my sister the witch she takes life like a joke, like game. A game of life where they do whatever they want, when they want and don't even care. Yes, blood is thicker than water. But that has to be proven to me because I don't believe in it. I would love to but it is too painful for me to understand.

How could I sit there like it was all OK? She thought wrong and I did not play her game.

It was Christmas Day morning about 6am and Jordan had opened up all his presents. It was not a lot but in a way it was a good job he was only four years of age. I felt really bad but I could not do any more than what I did. I tried my best, and that's what counts, and he loved the little lorries etc. Jordan would keep going upstairs to show his Dad his presents. Sometimes they would let him in but seven times out of ten he tried, they would not.

At midday, Peter's Stepmom came around to give Jordan his present. When she came she said, "God I did not think it had got this low." Jordan had hardly anything. I agreed with her. I told her Peter was in bed with my sister and she asked to take Jordan out for a few hours. I was very grateful to her. I felt so bad. Peter just cares for himself and keeps taking my money. Like it's his right. God, he made me feel sick. They both have got sick and twisted minds.

When Jordan came back we both watched Titanic. Actual I enjoyed my day with Jordan. I pretended to elf. Different things because of Peter and Stef. I did not show my son any sadness. None of this is his fault and I won't sit there and ruin his day because of the freaks upstairs. I will never forgive this and I never forget. Their black souls with their black hearts.

It just felt like my heart was going to explode and jump out. I could feel each beat. I carried on the day with Jordan. He had a bath around 7pm and bed after. I did not want Jordan to see my pain because of those pair of freaks.

I was lying there yet again trying to get to sleep and yet again the witch would come down. She loves to see me lower than her, hurt and sad. She loves to see that in me. She so enjoys to think she is in power. Power of this house and my life and what she said goes. I just looked at this soulless, cold-hearted person. Who is she really? This can't be my sister. Why does she want to hurt me so? WHY WHY WHY? 1 never hurt her hardly in life. She did me. All my life she hurt me and would be jealous of everything good in my life. Friends she took from me etc.

I hardened up a little come Christmas evening and just went with it. Like I had a choice. This was the second night they were in the bedroom together. Stef carried on being a witch. Somehow it did not take me long to get to sleep that night. Thank you, God.

I woke up and it was Boxing Day. My life, I think it was just a joke. It was a big joke on me. But why was this? Why did I deserve this? I did not understand how could get so much hate in my life. I loved people in my life, I thought when you care for someone in life You act like you do. Not betray them because they are a good person. I know now that they are heartless. . But heart is not to be wasted, I know this but you only give it to some person you think deserves this, but if this is not to be, please do not take all the blame You had love in your heart. But they only had jokes betrayal and hurt and heartlessness.

How long can a heart hurt for? How does a person deserve this much sadness? Please God, what have 1 done to deserve this much sadness? I'm so sorry God please believe me.

How much could they hate me? Why in their hearts did they do this to me? WHY? They knew I was downstairs but they just carried on doing whatever they were doing. Very cruel people. I could never do what they have done to me, even to get them back, I could not do such a cruel act.

It was later that day. I woke up on the settee. Jordan was watching TV. He asked why his Daddy was in bed with Auntie Stef still.

I said, "Do you know what, duck, I don't care! Please don't worry about them, sweetheart. Let's watch the cartoons, because they are cool and funny." So Jordan carried on watching TV. I got up and made a cup of tea. But while in the kitchen I was crying so much. My heart? Where has it gone? It hurts so much. But I can't let my son see me upset. So, I made a cuppa and had a fag. I just carried on and on like it did not bother me.

You need to be strong for your kids. You show them courage, love and feelings.

I needed to show my son what his Dad had done the past three days was not right. But my son was too young to understand. Jordan looked up to his Dad. How dare he show my son this!

The thing is I needed to show myself also. That

I knew Peter went with other women, that it was unforgiveable to do it like this and not even care how J felt. How can this man really care for me? He does NOT.

For the first time in all these years I knew Peter did not really love or care for me. Why has it taken so much to realize? I kept fooling myself. Pretending everything was OK and it was far from the truth. It's because when you love them and really love them with all your heart. I knew I did not deserve this much hurt. Finally, I understand! Wow, I'm such an idiot. But I believed in love and should not tell myself that was wrong. But loving and caring for someone who hurts you so much is wrong. But I did not seek the truth. How long can I keep fooling myself?

This was messing with my son's life. This is not what I wanted my son to see and learn in life. This was wrong. The courage I built up for my son. To save my son. That's what's important now. I can't be selfish to my son. This is not the life I want to show my son. I won't let my son see this selfishness in life, unless he will be the same. I need to hit the road Jack and NEVER come back. My son was already really naughty with me. Peter was telling him not to do what I say. I knew running away would be the easy part. Bringing him up on my own is the real challenge here. It was about 2pm when my sister came down the stairs and went out of the front door.

CHAPTER 18

I hated my life

She just slammed the door. Not long after, Peter shouted at me. I thought "Oh God, what have I done now?" As he shouted at me my stomach turned. I went up trying not to panic. I was so disgusted with him and my sister. I walked into the bedroom and sat on the side of the bed where I normally sleep and the sheet on the bed was covered in baby oil. I just sat there. My heart was hurting so much. I asked Peter why all the baby oil was on the bed and he replied, "What oil?" He said he did not know what I was talking about and it must be the sheet. I just swallowed so hard. How could he expect me to believe that? How does he expect to get away with this? Does he think I'm that stupid? I asked him why he was in bed with my sister for three days? He said "Don't go on."

When his friends knocked on the door and I said he was upstairs in bed with Stef they just looked at me. I think they thought I was just joking. But when his friends came back down the stairs to go they would just look at me shocked and stunned. Even though they just said bye. The look on their faces said it all.

Peter expected everything to carry on like normal. Like I said, "idiot man"!

I said, "It's unforgiveable of you and her. Why have you got me back for something I have not done. So, you did it all for nothing and it was very cruel of you."

I got up and walked downstairs. I told Peter how I felt, but not shouting. Just as gentle as I could. He could see he had hurt me a lot because I was saying it as I was crying.

He said, "Whatever!"

How could he? I'm sick of it all. How dare he treat me and his son in a way like this. I still can't believe what had just happened. I'd been in a daze for the past three days. Pretending in my head. Playing games, myself so it did not hurt me so much. But it did. pretending did not stop the pain and it never will. At least when he went with other women, I did not see them. But in the same house. God, I can't believe it.

I went back upstairs to Peter after I had a cuppa.

"Get undressed!" he said to me.

"What?"

I could not bear this. I couldn't say no to him because he would beat me up. He will think I'm going with someone else. So I had no choice but to have sexual intercourse with him. After, I had a bath and got dressed and cried my eyes out. I felt like an unpaid prossie!

But I still loved Peter. But he will never love me as much as I would like. Your body is your temple. I won't let him do this to me anymore. I feel dirty and nasty. I feel sick with myself. Why can I not say "no" if I don't want to do anything with Peter or for Peter. I just want to stick my middle finger to him and say, "Suck on this, prick head!" Idiot man.

It would be great. But even though I could not stop laughing at myself, I was just day dreaming. It can't hurt dreaming. One day they might come true. You never know!

All my life I've had to fight it. I would always be so positive before I met Peter. I was going to travel the world and try to be happy. I can't believe the life I've really had. It is nothing like I wanted or dreamed about. I hoped better for myself. I hoped better for my son. I hoped better for life, to live life.

I have got to do better for my son. The hate just builds up so much. I soon will be strong enough to go with Jordan. Sly courage was for my son.

Every day I would think of Peter and my sister in bed. Then after he went to bed with me. I want to have a choice not to obey like a dog. I would tell Peter it really hurt me what he did, plus he brought other girls back too, not so long ago.

Peter asked me to marry him. I was so happy. Peter gave me a ring from a can of coke because he had no ring. Right, I thought I'm so happy now. I've waited so long for him to ask me. I will push everything away because of the love I had for Peter. Jordan will have a Mum and a Dad who were married. Like it should be. I always wanted to get married with the person I had a child with. I'm old fashioned like that, you see.

Well my life is great, so I would pretend to myself. I told Jordan we were getting married. Jordan said, "Wow!" I laughed and gave him a hug. I so wanted for Jordan to have both parents. Like every child deserves. Peter even told one of his friends in front of me. It was great.

"You think I'll marry you?" Peter said a few days after. "I will never marry someone so thick as you. You thicko!"

I had been tricked again. I thought Peter would not pretend to marry me but he did. He knew how happy I was, but he stepped on my dreams again and they are nowhere in sight. My light at the end of the tunnel has gone. J felt like a fool for the millionth time. He just ripped out my heart and jumped on it. The pain I could not stand any more.

Peter started saying he was the Devil's helper and he would beat me up and the next morning he would try to pretend he knew nothing about my bruises. He would look so shocked. Saying he was going to kill the person who did this to me. He would keep asking who did this to me. I did not lie to him. I tried to explain to him it was him, but that he kept saying he was the Devil's helper. He would try to look confused like he did not realize what I was talking about. I just laughed inside. His temper was getting worse. I started to feel scared for my life. Peter was weird! I never realized how much of an idiot man he really was. Expecting me to believe him, he must have thought I was an idiot with him. How come I did not realize sooner?

When Peter was pretending be the Devil's helper he would pull a weird face and talk really creepy. It scared me. I had to go along with it otherwise he made me feel he would hurt me more. This was his only escape. It was not Peter that was hurting me. It was the Devil's helper. God, he acted the part really well. He told me my Mum was in hell. He came out with these creepy things. I wondered how he could say such things. His knowledge of things. The things he came out with were so scary. How did he know what to say and how to say it in such a way? I had been with Peter for eight years and yes he scared me, but him being the Devil's helper scared me to death. I was scared in a totally different way. I knew I could not cope with him anymore.

What was he going to come up with next?

I wanted to be gone so much. So I did. Two weeks after, me and my son escaped from him.

It had to be good for the escape plan to work. I asked the next-door neighbors to take us to the train station on the day. They said yes. I was so worried but knew it had to be done. Peter would have not expected the neighbors to help us. Right it was the last day before the escape. I was so nervous but I kept my cool for my son. I really didn't know if I could keep my cool. But I did keep cool. I was proud of myself and I thought "You go girl!" I would be talking to Peter and once I was out of the room I was out of breath scared. if this time was going to work.

Anyway I gave the neighbors some bags for me and Jordan the night before. I was shaking. I arranged with them to meet me and Jordan around the corner in the morning and I told Peter I was taking Jordan to school and then going to the post office. He said, "OK". Then I left the house. He did not mind that as it was the only time he did not mind me going out, every Tuesday morning. Because he thought he was going to get my money again.

I wanted to laugh but I did not dare. Because I knew my plans.

On the morning of the escape it was the hardest thing I had to do. Yes, I was scared. But my love for my son took over. I wanted to protect him from his twisted father. So I did.

CHAPTER 19

The escape

My neighbors put my bags in their car ready to go. God, my stomach was turning around so much with fear and excitement, and my head felt like it was going to go pop! God this is it. My plan has worked so far. Now it was to get in the car and get to Southampton.

I said bye to Peter. We were out of the door. As soon as Peter could not see us through the window I said to Jordan "Run!" We both got in the car and bent down in the back seat. I did not dare to move. Were my plans going to work this time? I was scared if they did and scared if they didn't.

We were in town waiting to catch our train to freedom. A road where I did not know what was going to happen next. Jordan was only four years old. He knew his Dad was nasty to me. But Peter was getting harder with Jordan. He started to smack him when he did not deserve it. Jordan may have done something wrong but did not deserve to be smacked the way Peter did. I was NOT having it. Sly son is my life. Whoever hurts my son, they hurt me too.

Sitting at the back of the car I would wonder about everything. Life without Peter. God, that is a dream. A dream that I wanted to happen for my son's sake. If we do get away this time, I will know dreams do come true. You have to work for it but YES dreams come true.

Please believe me. Abuse is wrong and we going to hit that road and NEVER come back. In my head I would be praying to God for us to get away my time.

We had to wait a few hours for our train. Time was going so slow. I thanked my neighbors for helping us.

They would hear me screaming and crying when Peter hit me. They understood why I needed to escape. Peter would never realize it was them who helped us. Right under his nose. I said, "In your face!"

Me and Jordan were on the train. It started to go. Wow I thought. It's worked, my plan actually worked! Hooray! I really just wanted to cry with happiness. What will life be like now? Peter? I was so scared of everything. I know I will try my best. That is all I knew.

We reached Southampton and jumped in a taxi to go to my sister's. Tracy was my older sister who decided she wanted to stay in Southampton after our Father passed away. She married a lovely man. She does not realize how lucky she is. Some people don't know what domestic violence is. They think they know, but they don't. My sister was just like that. Anyway, I had sent my post office book down to my sister to look after, which had money in the account and 100 loose in the book. I thought I was lucky to have a sister like Tracy.

I asked for my money and she passed me my post office book. There was no money inside. I asked my sister where it had gone.

"I spent it on the kids and paid off a phone bill with it."

"How dare you tell me you were coming down and didn't. So I spent your money. All the trouble I go to and you never turned up."

I could not understand d a right to why do what she did she this wants to me. She thought she had a right to do what she wants because she is helping me. I knew I would never forgive her she I was scared for my life every day. I could just walk out when I wanted. I don't understand why she did not know that. But she understood when she wanted to. Both of my sisters have chips on their shoulders.

It was the day after and myself and Jordan and Tracy went to town to try to get some help from the council. Vile went to the homeless section and explained why. They got me and Jordan in a refuge in Eastleigh, 10 minutes away on the train. The refuge was getting someone to pick me and Jordan up at Eastleigh train station but had to wait for the next day. I felt really nervous about it all.

The thing was I could not understand why my sister took my money. She was there when I was explaining about Peter. But she still said she was in the right for me letting her down and not arriving when I said I would. Why did she have to be so heartless? She knew I was heartbroken and she even said if I did not get out of it all when I did I would probably come out of that house in a wooden box. So why act so selfish? We only had my sister for help and she knew it. But yet she did this. WHY?

She hurt my feelings and we were only in Southampton less than 24 hours and she could see how upset and nervous a person I was, and yet she still took advantage. UNFORGIVEABLE!

That night we all got a Chinese. I made sure I put my money in for it as she might have thought I was using her. I also bought a bottle of wine to say thank you for helping me and Jordan.

But the thing was I should not have to think and worry about what she might be thinking and I should not have felt she thought I was using her. I thought I knew my older sister Tracy, but for her to take my money like that, she was not the person I thought she was. Yes, I was very grateful to her for helping us, but felt like I had to lick her feet because she did. She showed me what kind of person she really was.

Why do people treat me like this? I'm sick of feeling useless and like I am being bullied, but can't say anything because according to them I was the one in the wrong. But deep down I knew it was them.

That night after the kids went to bed, myself; Tracy and her husband had a couple of glasses of wine each. I felt nervous because when she has a drink she gets gobby. Not her husband though. Tracy would try to make me feel more useless by trying to put me down. She tries to make herself feel good about herself by putting other people down. I was not any good at trying to answer back. I forgot the last time I stuck up for myself. But yes, she did it again to me. I felt like I was an idiot. She made me think I was.

In the end her husband said, "Easy, stop talking to her like that, it's not fair."

Tracy did not like this. I always got on with her husband. From the time I met him a few years earlier. But I thought it was nice I got on with him. I got on better with him than I did my own sister. But Tracy I think was jealous of the fact. She treated me like I wanted to run off with him. I thought no, my name was not Stef! She did not want to admit she was in the wrong so she treated me like it was me. I only Wanted help from my big sister. That's all.

It was the next day and I woke up nervous and gutted about the way my big sister was like towards I was really quiet that morning and could not wait to get out of her house. I hardly spoke to her husband after that. I dare not to because of Tracy. By then they had five children together. I was proud of my sister and yes, I thought she was lucky to have a husband like him. But I would not want to do so much damage to the family. I know what that was like so I did not do it to other people; never mind my sister! I felt like she took me for a tart, to be jealous like that. But I knew I was not.

I only had my sister Tracy and felt like I had to think what I said before I said it because of the way she was. She was not a normal sister but neither was my twin sister Stef.

Me, Jordan and Tracy walked down to the train station with all my bags. I felt like I was going to the other side of the planet. I felt all alone.

CHAPTER 20

Our new lives

We got off the train at Eastleigh and just waited at the entrance where they would pick us up from. I brought a newspaper that morning, to remember the day. But I did not want to go back to Peter. I still have that newspaper 14 years on.

So, there we were waiting and the lady walked up to me.

"Are you Karen?"

I said, "Yes."

I felt nervous. Her name was Sarah.

"Don't be nervous, you're being very brave to do this."

"Thank you."

She said, "No problem" and we got in the car.

The refuge was only about two minutes down the road. God, I thought, a new road to my new life. Oh my God, I was screaming and crying inside. I only wanted the best for my son and to do good in life without being hit every day and bossed around like I was a dog. If I stayed with Peter, I dare not think about what Jordan would have been like by now. escaped and never went back to Peter but I wanted to, but did not for my son. It was the best thing for him. Your kids come first. all We got to the refuge and Sarah was showing us around. She took us up to our room. It had a lock on the door so our stuff was secure, and did not have to about our things being nicked. The little things worry did have.

Sarah showed us the back garden. It was quite There was another lady playing with her little big. girl. She asked me to look after her daughter while she went to the toilet. Me and Sarah looked at each other as if to say "She was cheeky, only being there ten minutes.'

I said OK to the lady and Sarah said to me, "Start as you mean to carry on." In other words, don't be taken for an idiot.

I had only been there five minutes and I felt like I had been taken for a fool already. I said to myself, "I won't say yes again to her."

It was getting late in the day and I needed to get some food. So myself and Jordan went down the road to Aldi. I had never been there before. But as long as they sold food there I did not care. It felt great this time, I was carrying bags of food just for me and Jordan. Whilst walking back to the refuge I was hoping and praying to God that I would never go back to Peter.

It felt strange that day going to bed, not having to worry about Peter or my sister Tracy. I felt happy even. This was a new start for me and Jordan and I was not going to waste it.

I woke up the next morning, I needed to get Jordan in a school. The helpers in the refuge helped me with that. We phoned up the school and then went around the next day to enroll Jordan in the primary school. It was great. Things were looking up.

At the refuge there were a couple of other women but I could see they had more faces than Big Ben! So all it really was, was "Hi, hope you're OK." Down south it was much warmer than up north. The sun was out and when Jordan went to school I would be sitting in the back garden and trying to keep busy. I phoned my sister Tracy up a few times and arranged to go and see her during that week. The two-faced woman she is. But she was all we had. There was no one else. Even though we got in the refuge and we were safe, I felt so alone and I was the only person in the world with a heart. Except the refuge workers of course!

I hoped when I came away from Stoke that Jordan was going to start to be a good boy. But even though he was four years old, God he could be naughty. I started to get worried about Jordan and what he was going to be like with me when he got older. I just hoped he would change now it's just him and me. It was all Peter's fault. He kept telling Jordan not do what I told him to.

The after effects of domestic violence, they never stop. Goes going on and on and on.

If only I was strong enough right at the beginning when I saw the signs.

We would be walking down the road and he would be shouting at me. He made me feel so low and embarrassed. But it's my fault my son is like this. I wished I never stayed with Peter at the beginning. My son might have had a different life where he had a loving Dad and loving husband to me. Just think, if only I realized when the signs were there. I took no notice. Now look at the life I've got. I have got nothing but my aching heart.

I got a voluntary job in Jordan's class, I loved it but when it started to become really sunny and warm stopped it. Sometimes it was nice just to sit in the sun in the back garden while Jordan was at school. sometimes a nice break too. We had now been in the refuge a few weeks. Jordan was still being naughty for When we would sit with the other women at the table at meal times, it was always Jordan who would be naughty. He would sit at the table eating like a horse. 1 would ask him to stop making noises when eating, but he would just carry on. Since it was a few weeks since we were there people started to get fed up with him. It did not matter how many kids there were, it was always Jordan who would be the naughty one. He would want my attention 24/7. So much patience. God, I so wished for him to be a good boy. But Jordan had been through a lot himself. I knew why he was naughty but no one else saw it that way. People started to moan about how naughty he could be.

There was a new lady who came in the refuge. Her name was Anna. She was from Reading and she had a three-year-old boy and a twelve-month-old baby boy. She seemed to be run down like me and did not wear make-up etc. "I'll show you where to do your shopping," I said.

She said "OK."

It was great, I thought I had a new friend and Jordan had a play mate.

But no, Jordan would be naughty which encouraged the other kids to be naughty as well. But if I went to the shop and I was not there he would be a good boy for them. As soon as I would get back he would start to be naughty again. So Jordan knew what he was doing, when he would be naughty. He also showed Other people he knew what This he ruined was doing, a lot so of it things used to upset people and me. for us. But all of it was the after effects of domestic violence. How long will it carry on for? That is like asking how long a piece of string is, when you can't find the end.

I want people to realize how much it does affect your children, when you are in a domestic violence relationship. Realizing things sooner will stop a lot of heartache. Please don't end up like me. I have nothing or no one. Please read this book and learn from it. Yes, I saved my son's life by saving him from his Dad, but he will still suffer like me for the rest of his life and all the heartache could have been avoided if I had read the signs. I'm asking you and praying for you to listen to me and learn from this book. PLEASE!

Anna had a brother, his nickname was Sav. I needed to get some of my stuff which was still in my house in Stoke-on-Trent. Anna asked me if it was OK she would ask her brother Sav to help me. I said yes and waited for her to let me know what he said. He agreed to take me to Stoke in his van and back for 00. I said "Really?" Anna said he will take me up and get some of my stuff and then after I could go and take my stuff to her house in Reading. He arranged it will be 50 for petrol there and back. It was so super cool of him. Also Anna. I was very grateful.

It was arranged that Anna would look after Jordan for the day and night.

Anna said Sav liked me and I also said I thought he's funny. But I did not fancy him. Really I just wanted my stuff. But I did think he was a nice person to talk to. But I was not ready to settle down yet and I don't think I ever will. But a bit of fun on the way won't hurt, haha!

CHAPTER 21

Memories

On the day of going to Stoke, I felt excited but nervous too. I had to meet Sav at 7am and he was going pick me up. Marcus, Sav's nephew, Anna's little boy, came with us too.

Once we got to Stoke it was arranged for us to go to the police station in Hanley, so the police helped us. We got to my old house and had to sit outside for 10 minutes while waiting for the council to come and take the big metal door down. Once it was open I ran in there. It was my house and my home before Peter ruined everything. Going through my stuff, God the house was in such a mess. I could not get a lot of stuff. I had to take the things which were needed the most. I felt upset and I had to run around too quickly, just in case Peter saw us. Also, to tell you the truth, I was scared too. But I needed some stuff. When I put the last thing in the van and shut the doors, I felt so upset. This house was my new start in life. I had it all taken from me like normal. God, my heart was hurting.

Memories! The lamp post which was on the corner of the road where I used to live, I was walking Jordan home from school when I put him on my shoulders and walked into the lamp post. The day I did that was really embarrassing but funny.

I had to try to leave all the memories behind, but I knew I would not be strong enough to do that. I loved Peter so much but now I hated him and I love him but not in a personal way, just friends. I could never forget my life with him. Before we drove away I needed just one more look at my house and the garden. I walked around to the back of the house. So many good memories with Jordan in the back garden. I had a few tears in my eyes because it was not fair. Heartache after heartache and on and on. Why did this have to happen to me? I ran back to the van and got in and shut the door. I looked up to the bedroom window where I used to look out of from the inside, wondering if ever we were going to be free one day. And look at me now. I looked at my house for the last time and blew it a kiss, saying "Goodbye". We drove off and I was just looking out of the window as my house got smaller and smaller until it was gone. I knew from that day I would never be back. Too much pain.

Sav asked me if I was OK and I replied "Yes". I was getting worried that if we were any longer Peter might have turned up. So I said goodbye to my house and said bye to Peter too.

We got to the bottom of the estate, Bentilee, and also said "Goodbye" to my Mum and my Stepdad's house at the bottom of the estate. I felt hurt and upset. Only sad memories, when does it stop?

Yes, we learn from life and learn from our mistakes, but when does the pain stop?

We got to Hanley and were feeling hungry, So Sav parked up on the side of the road where the chip shop was and I ran in and got chips and chicken, mmm the chips were yummy!

Soon we were out of Stoke-on-Trent. My home town. A lot of things and memories which needed to be forgotten, but it was not that easy for me.

By the time I finished my chicken and chips we out of Stoke-on-Trent. God, it hurt. But was it for the best or was it meant to be to be able to save my I think it was a bit of both.

It was another four-to-five hours drive back to Reading, then back to Southampton. It was so kind of Anna saying I could store my stuff at her house until I got a place to live. She was still going to be in the refuge for a while anyway. I felt happy but sad, but the main thing was Jordan will be OK and not be like his Dad. But was it too late? Jordan was already four years old. Peter had drummed it in his head to be naughty for me and not to do anything I asked him to. Jordan was still acting like that at five years, then six years and so on. He was getting naughtier and naughtier. I saw the signs that he was not going to be good for me and that he would get worse and to start hitting me. I hoped and prayed he would not be like that. I was scared and worried and dreading it. Please, please God. I hope he will NOT become his Dad.

Anyway, we got to Reading and put my stuff in the hallway of Anna's house. We went to McDonalds after. Then it was on the way to Southampton. Hooray! I sort of missed Jordan and could not wait to get back to see him. I took my TV and belongings to the refuge, as much as I could. I also got the photos of Jordan when we went to Olan Mills. They were lovely photos.

The next day waking up to my stuff and TV made me feel homelier in our room. It was nice. Well a lot better now. It was so nice just to be able to get some of our stuff. It came to all of this because I ignored the signs at the beginning of mine and Peter's relationship.

That he was a bad apple. There is a reason you get shown when a man is a bad apple — it's up to you. You have a choice. You either go down another road and leave them or carry on the road to hell. Well that is what it feels like. Please make the right choice in life and always remember to have respect and dignity for yourself and if someone doesn't like you, well it's their loss, not yours.

Well the thing is, nothing is ever that easy for me!

Me and Jordan carried on going to visit Tracy, nicknamed 'The Witch'.

Jordan would look forward to going and seeing his cousins, this was the only family we had. We would not want to ruin that. But Tracy seems to spoil everything. Tracy had six boys. All of them like to wrestle like boys. But one of the twins started to hurt Jordan for real because Jordan got the better of him when playing wrestling. I told my sister Tracy and I could not believe the reply.

She said, "If Jordan is going to start it, my boys will finish it. It's his own fault he got hurt."

I said, "But we are family and it should make a difference. Jordan loves coming to see them but not to get bullied."

I could not believe my ears when Tracy said that. I stopped the fight and Jordan was so upset. I could not and will not ever forgive her for being like that. Family is family. But not to her. I also hate her for some things she said. She once said that our Dad was not really my

Dad because I did not live with him. I said I get your point (but I did not) but yes of course he was our Dad too. I wanted cry for what she said. Was I supposed to agree with everything she said? In her eyes she doesn't do anything wrong. That is why I call her 'The Witch'. In your face!

Jordan would ask Tracy if he could sleep and camp out with the boys in the back garden but she would "No sorry, not got enough blankets". Again and again I could not understand her hatred for us. The weekend after Jordan asked, the boys had a friend each to camp with in the back garden, but they could sleep. Why on earth couldn't he? She would say no again. It was not fair on Jordan. I really felt for Jordan because he looked up to his cousins and he would have enjoyed camping out with them. That made Jordan really upset. It was not fair of her at all. Now I call her 'Devil woman' also.

It used to really upset me the way Tracy was. I went to visit her, like I normally did on a Tuesday. We would go to the charity shops to see what bargains we could get. I used to really look forward to going. But one week I went, I left my money on her table in her front room. I did not realize until halfway to the shops. Not long before she'd had a little boy called John. I explained how sorry I was but she would not stop shouting at me, like I did it to upset her. I just left my money. She said she had to feed John on time, how dare you upset me like this, I kept saying sorry to her. But she just seemed to ignore me when I was saying something. She stormed back to her house like a little child, pushing the pram. I'm so sick of her. I was her sister not her dog.

We got to the bottom of her road. I said I would run up and get my money instead of her going, but she said no, she would go because she did not trust me enough to have her key. So I waited at the bottom of her road and let her carry on. Whilst I waited for her I had a fag. She made me feel really upset. I did not mean to leave my money on her table. So there I waiting for her to come back and she stormed back.

"You bitch for not walking up with me," she shouted.

"But I said I offered to go and you said 'no'!"

But she did not care. She shouted at me like I a little child. Whilst she was walking she would turn around and say how could I do this to her. I said 1 did not mean to. At this point I could not stop crying whilst walking down the road. She did not care. She also called me a "cry baby".

This was very cruel of her. She thinks she is in the right with what she said to me. But it's NOT. She is the nasty one, and blames everyone else for her mistakes. So it looks like I'm the cruel one and I deserved to be called a bitch. She hurt my heart so much that day. How could she. Blood means nothing to her. I lost contact with her from that day for another few months. I will never forgive her, never ever!

I got home that day and just cried, how can my sisters keep treating me like this? Were they really my sisters? I knew they were, but they hardly acted like it.

Anyway we had been in the refuge two months now. I applied for a flat in Southampton. I could not wait for that day when I get a letter to say I got one. Everyone in the refuge was acting a bit rude towards me and Jordan because Jordan was always naughty. But you would think when you are in a refuge, why are you there? The way I got treated by Peter, I don't think the other women in the refuge had it as bad as me, because they would have understood about Jordan being naughty. We all used to have meal times together but it got to a point no one would sit at the same table if myself or Jordan was there. It was not very nice and it made me and Jordan feel more out of place. I think the refuge workers could see everything. I think they pushed it more so that I got a place sooner, because they could see how we were being treated by the other women.

CHAPTER 22

A new start

S o I had my sister upsetting me and the other women at the refuge acting funny with me too.

The days were getting longer, nobody would really talk to me in the refuge. One morning I got the post, got my two letters I had and left the rest on the table for everyone to see their post. I went upstairs to my room, not opening any of my post. I lay on my bed not knowing what to do in life. After a few hours I opened up one letter and it said I had got a maisonette in Bitterne in Southampton. Wow, thank you God!

I ran down the stairs to the refuge workers in the office. Showing them the letter, they could see how excited I was. Great, I thought out of this place. Woman are too bitchy with one another. Why? I don't know. I say life's too short. Anyway, I was holding in my hand my new home, my new life. How exciting! I needed to apply for a loan to get some help with getting some stuff from the social. I had nothing but a TV and clothes.

It was funny really. As soon as people knew we were going, they started to be nice again. Like I said they've got more faces than Big Ben.

It was the morning we were moving to our new home. Super cool! Sav was coming later with my stuff from Anna's house in Reading. Me and Jordan were happy. Hooray!

Getting our stuff together I could not stop smiling. I so wanted to do well and try to do the best for my son. Both of us deserved to be happy. Well happy here I come!

On the way to my new home I could see how happy Jordan was. He was excited, it was nice to see. I loved him so much and I preferred to see him with a happy face. My little darling!

Oh my God, we are here! But the only thing that was there were three lots of stairs to walk up every time, to get my stuff for my new home. I thought all the bad bits, it was worth it to be here now. My son's life was saved and if I had to sit on my own for the rest of my life, it was all worth it for my son. I love you, I love you, I love you.

Anyway, it was the first day in my new home and new life. The sun was out. It was nice. Hooray! My new life, here I come.

It was a Saturday morning, I did not have to take Jordan to school so we had a lazy day, waiting for my cooker, fridge freezer and washing machine to come. I already paid for them to put the cooker in for me so all I had to do was wait for them to come and they were going to do the rest, so not to worry about that and think about this day. It took me years to get here and I did it. My son's life has been saved. It's because he is my beautiful darling son of mine. He is gorgeous too.

It was Monday morning and I took Jordan to school, which was a task on its own. I knew the school was close by. But I had no clue how to get there. So I followed a man taking his little girl to school. Well, she was in a uniform with a book bag. So yes I followed this man and crossed my fingers it was the right school. What was I to do on the way back. Oh my God, nothing is ever easy for me!

Well at least I got to him to school and if I had to camp out because I was lost, at least I got him there. I was worried how to get back. But I did it, thank you God!

Well the early morning task was done, what next, I wondered?

One thing I was worried about was Jordan. He became even more naughty. I was trying to do my best with him. I did not realize that by me giving in to him already, it was not really teaching him respect. He knew what it was, but more and more he treated me with less and less respect.

By Peter telling me I wouldn't be able to look after him I gave him too much and he thought his opinion counted but he was only a child. I was trying to become his friend. But between kids and adults there should be a boundary, but with me and Jordan there was not one. By this time, Jordan thought what he says should go. That was wrong of him. But this is why I talk about the circle of hope and the effects of domestic violence. It goes on and on. But I had to suffer this and it's all Peter's fault. He taught Jordan from an early age to do nothing I say. So thinking about everything as Jordan was getting older, things were getting worse with him as well. This is why I should have realized and got out of the relationship before I had children. You think by having a child thing will become better but they don't.

Bringing up children in a domestic violence relationship is unfair to them and to yourself.

When you think about it, it's just an innocent person like yourself. You will be putting them through the hell you go through. Please,

please think about it. Your partner is a heartless person and very selfish.

So if you have a child, it's less time for them. They want all the attention. Think about it. So please, please having children doesn't help, they will just suffer like you. If they say they want a baby with you, it's because they want to trap you, and that is not a good thing either.

Not all children, but when they grow up in a domestic violence household they can become abusers themselves. How would it make you feel knowing your children are the same, it.would hurt you. So PLEASE think about it.

Sometimes, whilst thinking about my life and actually what people can be like, all the heartless people should be put on a desert island and treated like prisoners. That's how we get treated. It's just fair! We go through it and so should they too. But face facts, it's not going to happen, but it would be nice if it did!

Bringing up Jordan, the only thing he went without was family. I had a twin sister that took drugs and was so selfish and untrustworthy, and another sister who made us feel not welcome, it would have been nice if Tracy even just invited Jordan around her house. No, she just made excuses when Jordan wanted to sleep as always. So me and Jordan felt so alone. I do think if we had family that loved us our lives would have been better. We were so lonely.

Jordan also started to become more protective of me. He did not like me to have friends and as soon as I did have a friend he would start to become more naughty for me so people would get pissed off and stop being my friend. Peter said he would do this to me. So he taught Jordan from birth to upset me as much as he could and blame me for their mistakes

With what I went through with Peter I did not like going out, it was like I was scared too. I felt so useless and like I was an idiot. But I truly knew I was not one. I thought I looked like one and if anyone looked at me in the shops or anywhere I thought they were looking at me because I was an idiot. I was worried about everything. I would not flush my toilet after 10 pm every night in case I made too much noise for the neighbors and thought I would get into trouble. I was not used to having a life or anything.

I used to go out every Tuesday to do the shopping. I would get all the food for the week and pay the bills for a week and get back in. I only went out after to take and bring Jordan back from school. I did not dare to wear something that showed off my arms so I would cover all my body even in the summer.

All I seemed to do was cry. I'm good at that. Life is good for some people, but life has just been too hard for me. It did not matter what good I tried to do, I have always had to suffer.

Soon Jordan will be five years. I love my son so much but he had to suffer himself. Having no family really hurt the both of us. Christmas day we would both cry because it was just the both of us. No family. Some people take their family for granted, but it's like a jewel, to treasure what you got and each other.

Every Saturday there would be wrestling on TV, so Jordan would get carried away and head lock me and jump on me. It was so funny. M/e would get the cushions off the settee and put them on the floor. In the end, I got Jordan a big teddy bear so he could try to head lock it and not me. Jordan was only five but God he was getting bigger and stronger. The little devil.

For his sixth birthday Jordan had a party. There was ball pit etc. for them to play on after. Jordan was really excited when inviting all his friends. It made him happy and it was lovely to see him happy and enjoying himself. Jordan made a few friends. Could see Jordan enjoyed his party, I'm glad he did. He did not have to tell me that he enjoyed himself, I could see it. That made me feel happy for myself and for him. We had a lift home, it was great, no buses, as I was tired. I just wanted to get in and have a cuppa.

I always thought of Peter when good times happened and what he missed out on watching Jordan growing up. It was a shame for them both. And for me too. I wanted more children and to get married and stay with that person for life. But no that was not meant to be.

Even though I was a single parent, I think in my eyes Jordan got spoilt. But I might be comparing my childhood against his, also spoilt with the love I showed him. But being a friend does not help. He grew up thinking he had a right to say what he said and it meant to go in his head. But trying to tell Jordan what he said as a child and not an adult does not go. Peter has a lot saying for him. This is why Jordan is bossy and thinking how he thinks is right.

CHAPTER 23

Jordan

Jordan would say he hated me. But if only he knew the truth. But he was too young to realize, or was he? He blamed me for everything. That is why Jordan would say he hated me. But like myself I wanted family and so did Jordan. I don't blame Jordan for hating me. I think I would if I was him. But as an adult, I expect him to realize the truth. I wish he does one day and he doesn't hate me. But I've just got to wait and it hurts me. All of this is because of Peter. When I saw the signs at the beginning I should have run as far as possible, but I didn't and now look. All this heartache.

Day after day it was the same routine. I started to think about where I grew up and the people I left behind. I had started to talk to Peter's brother's girlfriend. I always thought she was my friend, but in the end, she was not either. But I thought I could try to get in touch with her but I did not know how. Then I remember that her stepdad went into a bookies and I knew where. So I got the number and left a message at the bookies for him.

A week later he phoned me. I could not believe it and it went from there. I spoke to Tina and I arranged to go up to see her. I could not wait. I missed my home town and it was dead exciting for me. I was thinking of going to see my Mum and I wanted to try and find my Stepdad. But was it better if I just let sleeping dogs lie? I did not know. Until I got up there.

It was a couple of weeks before I went to Stoke. Wow, I thought. Jordan was happy too about going. But I think I expected too much. It was never good living in Stoke before I left. I don't know why I thought it was going to be different now. But I knew there was something about Tina I did not trust. Tina had a loving mum and stepdad and had a family to help her. But I never had anyone. She wanted things her own way too much. I think she was very spoilt by her family. She did not realize that what she took for granted I wished for. She did not realize what she had. Spoilt, that's why. There was nothing wrong about that, but I felt it was or she was not fair with me. That is why we are not friends today and don't think I ever want to talk to her again. She's not the friend I thought she was. She also hurt me. A real friend would not have done that.

So staying in Southampton was good after all. I'm glad we never went back to Stoke to stay. So I carried on day in and out, doing the same old thing. I felt like I gave up. And I'm not a giver-upper. I can't give up now. I may have no family or friends but I will fight and fight and fight. I will show my son what life is all about and hope he is wise enough to use this knowledge. He's a fighter too. He may not realize it, but he will as time goes by.

Jordan's birthday was in the school summer holidays. It was very hard trying to save money for day trips plus his birthday. I had no help with anything. Due to his birthday being when it was, it was very hard for me. I wanted to do so much with him, but could not afford to. This I found was not fair on Jordan. We never went on holiday because I could not afford to, All Jordan's friends had family and people helping them but for me, it was just myself. I felt so bad for Jordan. He so deserved to have family and it would have been great for me too. Jordan, as he was getting older, felt upset about it all and this is why he blamed me for everything. I understood his pain but I could not always fix it.

After not talking to Tina for over a year I received a letter from her saying that she wanted to come to visit. I said yes. She was my best friend and I did not want to give up on her. She went through the same as me while she was with Peter's brother. This is why I did not understand why she treated me badly. I wished now I never bothered. Anyway, I phoned her and she came to visit.

It was alright for the first few days, but she got bored very easily. I did not have a lot to offer her. But what I offered as a friend was never good enough for her. I think she came down to give her something to do. Not to visit me or Jordan, not really. I could see she was not interested in us. She met one of the neighbors and she went to live with him. I could not believe it. This upset me and Jordan. She was bored with us so she went on her next adventure. I would see her around the school. It was a shame the way she was. Jordan would say that Auntie Tina doesn't love us anymore. I said to Jordan I was sorry.

But I knew the neighbor and he was up to no good. Tina thought she could use him. But I did wonder how long it would last. He was a player himself and I knew he would realize that about her.

Within a few weeks she came knocking at my door saying she split up with him and she was calling him names. I laughed inside. Now she wanted to talk to me. I let her in of course but she hurt me again and again. She said she wanted to go back home. I thought hooray! This was on the Monday and I did not have any money till Tuesday. So I had to knock on one of my other neighbor's doors asking them to lend me 5 till the next day. I never asked anyone for anything, but I had no choice. The neighbor said yes but it was in change. I thanked her and said it was very kind of her. The next day after I'd been to the post office I paid her back and invited her to come around. She said OK. When she came around Tina would always try to make me look stupid. So I felt really embarrassed. Anyway, she went the next day. Hooray!

CHAPTER 24

Making a new friend

I had made a friend, so one good thing came out of Tina visiting me, I thought. Her name was Clare.

She asked me about Tina and why she kept trying to make me look stupid? I said I didn't know and didn't care for her anymore. Like I said, if she was a real friend to me, she would not have kept hurting me as she did.

A few days went by when the lady next door came around and wondered whether I would like to go around hers one night and get a takeaway. I said yes, thank you. Clare, said the way I was treated by Tina was not fair. I just said I was glad she was gone. Clare said she wondered why! I just laughed. So me and Jordan went around that night and it went from there. It felt great to have a friend and only next door. Clare had a brother called Philip. He was pretty cute. I thought anyway. So I started to go around Clare's every day. Clare had not long started to drive. She had a blue Fiesta. Clare was married with two small ones. Philip was only 18 years old. But he acted more grown up than that. He did not smoke or drink. Clare and Philip did not have a good upbringing. Philip was brought up by his nan. He was a nanny's boy (spoilt). But with their mother running off on them when they were young, I think their nan tried to make up for it.

One night I went around to see Clare and Philip was there with his friend. God, I thought he was cute at this point I did not say anything to Clare, with it being her brother. It was a good night and I thought Philip was funny, cute and innocent looking. It was a good night and within a few weeks I was dating him. For once I felt happy and life was on the up. I could see Philip went through a lot as he was growing up and I think with me going through a lot too, it made us closer. I did not know what love was like real love anyway -- but he made me love again. I liked him so much.

Jordan though was still being naughty for me. I would watch him playing with Clare's little ones and he would try to trip them up and he did not like to share things. I felt like because of the way he acted he was going to spoil things like he always does, because he was jealous of everything I did or everyone I talked to. It was like he was obsessed with making my life hell. He looked like he enjoyed it when I was unhappy. But this was Peter's fault. These are the after effects of domestic violence which I will have to live with. If only I acted on it at the beginning I would not have gone through this and near my son. Jordan could not help being the way he did. But other people didn't see it that way. But I understood why he acted like this and I knew I would have to live with it too.

Philip tried so hard to understand this but it was hard for him. As time went on we split up over Jordan a few times. I was with Philip for six years off and on. If he went funny with Jordan. I went funny with him. I would not let him tell him off even though he deserved it. But Philip would use Jordan to start arguments. He was funny like that. Just because he wanted time out. It was too hard for him because Jordan would be so naughty. In the end we split up for good. My son had to come first.

So there I was on my own again. I decided I had to carry on fighting and not let the after effects control my life, which it did and always will. I started to college. It was so hard for me to go out of the door. I would have 100 fags before going. While walking to college I would pray to God to help me be stronger.

As time went by, Jordan started to throw things at me and would kick me when he did not get his way. I knew he would hurt me more as he was getting older and he would become stronger. I became scared of my own son. If a man looked at me and Jordan noticed, he would say it's because I looked like a tart. His words became more hurtful and the things he threw were getting bigger. I put a lock on my bedroom door because he thought he could go in my bedroom whenever he wanted to. In the end I would run upstairs to get away from him, when he scared me but he hit and kicked the door down and he would laugh because he could see I was scared. He looked like he enjoyed the power just like his Dad did. I would go to bed crying mostly every night.

I would be able to see the evil in him. He became his Dad. I would see Peter in his eyes. I became weaker and weaker with him. I wanted to make a good life for us but Jordan would not let me. After I finished college, I wanted to get a job but realized I could not because I did not have any help. I had to wait until he was older to get one. Until then I would have to carry on suffering. I hated my life. It was not fair. Life was not fair. I had no one to talk to, no one to help me. Just me, myself and I. Jordan would tell me he hated me and I deserved what he did to me. I would have bruises on me from the things he would throw at me. Yes, he was Peter in the end. He would laugh at me when he saw me cry. and call me a cry baby. He would say, «no wonder my Dad hit you.»

He would make me feel so small. But I had to live with this because I chose to ignore the signs from his Dad. I would see though that he was just hurting inside. But so was I. I would talk to Jordan telling him that what he does was wrong but he was too far gone. He seemed to think he was in control and I was the one who I had to do what I was told, not the other way around. Because it was only me and him while he was shouting at me, he looked like he was going crazy in his eyes. I did not know what I was going to do.

Jordan would shout at me like it was his right. But Peter told Jordan he had that right and it always stuck in his head. So it was not Jordan controlling my life it was Peter still. I knew that, but it did not help matters. Thinking my son was going crazy because he hated the fact it was just me and him. Life was too hard for him at such an early age. God, I hated Peter for this. But also I hated myself. For letting myself go through this. Jordan did not ask to be born and I felt like everything was my fault. Love has a lot to answer for. Why did I have to love Peter? I would have loved to get married and have more kids but I felt like I chose this life all because I ignored the signs at the beginning.

I found it hard to talk to people or trust people. Peter has destroyed my life and my dreams. But dreams can come true and I've got to remember that. Why can't I be happy. But it was nowhere in sight. I would try to grab it but I was too far away. Besides, Jordan would let me be happy. But knowing why Jordan acted the way he did, it did not make it better.

I knew I had to just sit it out until he was old to move out or something. enough

I could see the sadness in his eyes also. Trying to understand him and knowing why he is the way he is hurts my heart. He's my beautiful son. I would talk to him telling him the way he's acting is wrong. He knew it was but I don't think he could help it. His temper was just like his Dad's. How can he stop being naughty for me if his Dad taught him to be like this?

Knowing the position, I was in, I still tried not to give up. Jordan thought he knew it all about life, and he was very clever but at the wrong things. He would not listen because he thought he knew best. He did not know how to explain how he felt and because people knew he was naughty he would get the blame for things he had not done. All because he would not listen to me.

Once when my twin sister Stef came to visit me, I asked her to pick up Jordan for me from school. I wished I had never bothered to ask her now. But due to the fact she took drugs, she thought she knew best as well. But she embarrassed him and from that day on he got bullied at school. I could not believe it. I felt so bad and still do when thinking about it. I just wanted a little help and Jordan had to suffer for it.

After that, because kids will be kids, Jordan hardly had any friends. The only one time I asked my sister to do something for me and she had to embarrass him, God, why does life have to be so hard? Jordan was bullied all the time after that. I used to have bricks thrown at the window. I went to bed crying every night. I felt for Jordan and I hated my sister even more. She would never listen and still doesn't to this day. But in a way they were both the same' It was like he was her child not mine. He had the same attitude as her. They were both the same in many ways.

Stef would come around to visit me and nick my stuff just like she always had. She nicked from me as a child and still 30 years on she did. This hurt me while growing up and as an adult.

Arguing with Jordan because he would say nasty things to me was just like growing up with Stef again. Both of them thought they could say what they like and expect to get away with it. But the thing is both of them were the after effects of domestic violence.

My Mum still suffered. She suffered till the day she died. My Mum never got over the pain. But I don't think anyone gets over the pain. You have to live with it and accept it's there, but living with it you've got to try to cope with it. No, it's not fair, but you have no choice to.

But when I was little I didn't realize this and wondered why people acted the way they did.

I would go to visit Stef instead of her coming to my place, because I could not trust her. I hated her boyfriend because they would argue in front of me and he would slap her in front of me too. Then when they stopped Stef would blame me for why they were falling out. What? What did it have done with me? Stef would still blame things on me and not accept her Own mistakes were her own, not mine.

In the end, I stopped going to visit her because she would say I was seeing her boyfriend behind her back. I could not believe my ears. Once she called me a lot of nasty names because she knew all along I was with her boyfriend. I could not believe what was happening. Yes, she did it to me, but I was not the kind of person to get her back like that and do such a sick thing.

After I went to visit Stef, Jordan would start on me saying I drank etc. with Stef. He would kick off saying I wasn't allowed to see her because she was scum.

I could not win.

Jordan started to go out on a Friday and sometimes not come in till the Sunday night. He started to hang around with a gang which made me worry even more for him.

CHAPTER 25

Getting a job

I started to hate my life because I felt there was no 1love in it. I had no one really to talk to. So there I was crying my eyes out yet again after Jordan went to bed. I did not like to give up. So I passed my college course and thought I was ready to get a job. I applied for a few jobs and didn't get them, but then I had a telephone call from one of them saying to come for an interview. Wow, I thought, yes this was my break which I thought I deserved. It was being a career at an old people's home. I started part time and within six months I was made Senior. My life was on an up and I worked hard. But I still got Jordan hitting me and t. being nasty to me. I would go to work with bruises all over me, but I did not show anyone or tell anyone. Then one day I told my Manager, who I thought was lovely. I made friends with her daughter, Lucy, which was lovely too. I felt like I had a family, once again.

I made some friends and could not wait to finish work to see them. But after doing a 13-hour shift I could get very tired. I made one friend who was funny and he understood when I told him some personal stuff. I thought he was my friend, but in the end he was a nasty piece of work,

But before I was made Senior, Jordan was hitting me but I still had to go to work with a smile. Due to me going to work Jordan would not go to school most Of the time. It did not matter what I did, it was never good enough for him. But when I went to work Jordan would moan that I was out a lot but I was not I was going to work. One day when I was off work Jordan would not let me out of the door. He would stand in front of the living room door and not let me through it. In the end, he started to put knives to my throat or even try to strangle me.

The thing was I had to do the shopping on my days off. But that day I did get out in the end thanks to my neighbor. But I could see the madness in his eyes. I knew from that day I had to do something. I went to my old boyfriend Philip for advice and he calmed me down. I did not know what I was going to do. But while walking to Philip's I knew what needed to done. I went to the police and it was the second time I had done this. For my own safety, Jordan got placed into care. I could not believe everything was on the up. But Jordan got obsessed with me. But like I said, it was the after effects of domestic violence. I knew I could give him the help he needed. He was 14 years old and he hurt me a lot then. I was scared of him and he was getting bigger.

So with my son going into care and me being made Senior, everything was too hard to cope with. I lost my job within seven months. I felt like I had lost the world. I lost everything I worked for and wanted in life. I felt such a failure. I started to see more of my friend Tony, who I thought was a good friend, but he was just a player in life. Everything was a big game to him and his partner.

I went to live at his old flat for a little while because I felt like I could not live in my own home. But running away from your problems is not the answer. I learnt that the hard way. With staying at his flat for a little while I came to realize that Tony was not the really good friend I was hoping for. arranged with one of his friends who lived up north to go to visit for a couple of weeks. Just to help me because I was still low in confidence.

But the morning we were about to go Tony got drunk because he was jealous I would go with his friends. Tony said he liked me. But I said I only wanted to be friends. He does not know how much he hurt me by getting jealous. I knew he was gay, but he would say he wasn't. He lied about everything. Because he got jealous and got drunk he expected me still not to go. We went to the coach station and he was not allowed on the coach because he was drunk. He expected me to get off the coach but I stayed on. His face hit the floor. I knew he was not the good friend he kept telling me he was. If he was he would not have acted in such a way.

CHAPTER 26

Running from life

S o there I was on the coach going to a place I did not know and to a person I had only spoken to on Facebook a few times. Later that day, while still on the coach, I had a text saying that Tony had smashed up my place and all my things. I could not believe this. What kind of friend was he?

They said the cats went to a good home but I did not believe that. He probably just chucked them out on the street. That's what a heartless person is.

Well I arrived at Peterborough and I got my suitcase and just waited at the bus stop. I didn't know Tony's friend but I had seen a picture of him. I was just waiting for some man that looked like the photo. After 10 minutes I saw a small man who looked just like him. I said "Hello" and he asked me if I was OK. When I got back to his place, I found that he lived in a caravan and he had a dog named Candy and a cat named Charlie. His place was OK and he was OK, I thought. But yes, again that's what thought got me!

As the days went by I helped around his place but noticed he thought it was my job all the time. I did not realize at first that he wanted a slave. About four years previously he had a blood clot in his head. I come to realize he was OK if he was getting his own way. He thought J had no place to go and I had no choice but to stay there. He was a game player. God'

I was so wrong about him. I really thought he care for me. I did everything for him because I thought he was ill and he couldn't. But it was far from the truth.

After a few months of me being a slave and not realizing it, I tried everything in my power to make him happy. But yet again everything I did was never good enough. So I wanted a break from him and said I wanted to go and see my son for his birthday. I could not wait to go. He started to say I was using him. He got funny with me so I never ate at his place. I used to be starving. I would make him something to eat but not for myself. I was giving him money, but he said it was not enough and he was always moaning when I wanted a bath every day. He would moan that I was using too much electricity. I could not believe what was happening to me yet again. I fell for it again. I took the risk and wished I never had. A few days before I was about to go and see my son I told him I would be back in two days. Yeah right!

He was another idiot man! He pretended to take an overdose and blamed me for it. So instead of him blaming me all day, I got his friend's number and told him he took an overdose. I thought, you idiot man. I did not tell him I texted his friend and that he was pretending he took all these tablets and left a note. So I played back. In your face! He had no choice but to tell his friends what happened.

But his friends came with his wife and everyone knew I was a slave for him. She told him that he was a very selfish person to do this. He blamed me for everything but they knew he was full of it. In your face! A few days later I was gone. Hooray, I thought.

I went back like the fool I acted because I felt sorry for him. He kept saying on the phone that he had not eaten since I had gone because he couldn't do things for himself. So I felt guilty and went back. I told him I would only be there for two weeks at a time and then I would be going back to Southampton. He agreed with me, but really he did not. I arranged to take my cats and was really ready, I thought, to give up my flat for him, so I was able to look after him.

Every time I was due to come back I started to feel ill the day before. I did not realize he was poisoning me each time. So I was too ill to travel and then I would have to stay with him. This happened a few times. The last time I travelled to see him he poisoned me again and I was asleep for three days. I could not believe it. I felt so scared. I thought I was OK but he poisoned me again and I was sleep for another two days. I woke up and there was a ring of fire around me. He thought I was dead so he set the covers I was lying under alight. He went out to make out he knew nothing. I don't how I survived that day. Something woke me up and I put out the fire and went back to sleep. When he came back to see me asleep and the fire was out, he must have been gobsmacked. What an evil man. He tried to murder me twice.

When I woke up properly I was scared for my life. I was shaking and acted nervous. He could see this and acted stupid like he did not know what happened. That night I did not sleep. I lay on the bed awake all night scared for my life because he said he was going to blow the place up and we would die together. Oh my God, I thought. I did not know how to feel or what to think. I just could not believe I was so wrong about this evil man. Why me, I thought. Why can't I meet a good man and be happy?

I did not move all night and waited till sunrise and I got out of there. I ran for my life. I phoned 999 and they helped me to get to the train station.

I was able to get some stuff and one of my two cats. When on the way to the station I could not stop crying. When I reached Southampton I got a taxi back to my flat. I nearly gave up my flat for him. It's a good job I did not. I just sat there for a few hours thinking of what happened and thinking I nearly died. No way! M/as this a big joke on me? That was it for me. I was never going to go out with another man again.

I got settled in my flat even though I had nothing. I needed to get a washing machine etc., but it was better than with that idiot man. I was still breathing and that's what really mattered to me.

I was still missing Jordan as ever. I would not be able to sleep at night or couldn't go out to the shop even. My depression got a lot worse. I started to feel bad in the head. I would just stare at things, I felt like every bit of energy or life had just gone within me. I could not think or eat properly. Life felt too much. Every morning I woke up I wished I had not. Life was too much for me to handle.

I started to see ghosts. They were just walking up and down the street like the living do. Tell you the truth, I enjoyed it. Thought it was interesting. It was not scary for me like I thought it would be. But one night I looked out of my window to see something with red eyes just looking straight towards me. It scared me to death. I closed my curtains and covered the sides of the curtain so there were no gaps. I thought if I did that I was safe. I realized how the mind can play games on you. But seeing those red eyes scared me too much.

I needed to get stronger within myself because of what I had seen. I knew I was going to die. I had to wake up to myself and shake myself. Come on girl! Don't give up now! I would say to myself. Over and over.

The thing I hate is being so lonely still. Yes, I know I'm doing it for my son, but why do things have to hurt all the time? I feel like a failure. Weak and like a tramp. Every time I go out I see families, parents, grandads, grandmas. What about me? Don't I deserve a family? I need to make sure I tell my son my story, then he might talk to me. Well I hope, anyway!

Every time I was upset I would phone Tony. I really thought he was my friend and that he cared for me. I have not got anyone else. Tony drinks too much. I know what I had been through and it's not an excuse to drink all the time like he does.

Tony and Dave had nobody else either. Their families had given up on them both. I thought it was a shame as I knew how they felt, having no family myself. I tried to understand their behavior. Why would they both want to drink the way they do? I think it is because of life and the way life can treat you. It's not an excuse for drinking, but having no one there does hurt.

Tony would tell me he wanted to kill himself, He would knock on my door crying. But the thing was he was just pretending. Some of the time. He would say he can't live without me, if I fell out with him. He would write me letters. But in the letters he would sound like I was in a personal relationship with him. But I was not. He was fooling himself. God, he must be another nut job. Not again!

This went on for four years. When he came to visit me, he would need a shave and clean clothes on. God' his feet stank so much. It was disgusting. Anyway me being me, I would do him something to eat and make be married. God, my beautiful son, I'm so proud of him. My heart sank to the floor when she told me. But I wish him a good life and to be happy.

So I sit in my home waiting for Jordan to come back to me, day in and day out I wait.

I ever find love and happiness? Will my son ever come back to me? Is it only on TV when it's happily ever after?

www.ingramcontent.com/pod-product-compliance
Lightning Source LLC
Chambersburg PA
CBHW021636120626
46545CB00002B/569